In the pages of "The Narrow Path," Tara Chelioudakis clearly explains how New Age deception is connected to the New Apostolic Reformation (NAR) movement. From her testimony and expository writings supported by Scripture, Tara does an excellent job of identifying apostasy in the church today. I recommend this book for anyone who is involved with the New Age or NAR, or if you have a loved one in these movements. "The Narrow Path" can equip you with knowledge and awareness for the discernment of deception.

—Doreen Virtue, author of "Deceived No More"

THE
NARROW PATH

ESCAPING THE
GRIPS OF DECEPTION,
WHILE DISCOVERING
HIS WAY, LIFE, AND TRUTH

TARA CHELIOUDAKIS

Published by Author Academy Elite
P.O. box 43, Powell OH 43035
www.AuthorAcademyElite.com

Identifiers:
LCCN: 2019915155
ISBN: 978-1-64085-960-9 (Paperback)
ISBN: 978-1-64085-961-6 (Hardback)
ISBN: 978-1-64085-962-3 (Ebook)

Available in paperback, hardback, and Ebook

TABLE OF CONTENTS

PART 4: DOCTRINES OF DEMONS

CONCLUSION: THE NARROW PATH

DEDICATION

This book is dedicated to the ones I love the most: my four beautiful children, and my husband, who has always supported me. I pray that my story will touch them, and they will seek after truth in a world where many are blinded by deception. May Jesus lead them to the narrow path of life.

ACKNOWLEDGEMENT

First, I would like to thank and acknowledge my husband, who has been there for me through so many spiritual changes, has never doubted me, and encouraged me to share my story. I also would like to acknowledge Author Academy Elite for helping me write and publish my first book. A special thanks to my editor, Christy Stevenson Scott, for taking on this project. A very special thanks to my good friend and ex-New Age author, Doreen Virtue. Also, to Melissa Doughtry for supporting my book and allowing me to share my story through an interview that has reached many. And, lastly, I must thank Jesus Christ, my Lord and Savior for giving me the wisdom and strength to write this book and for surrounding me with a community of Christians who are all fighting for the same cause: TRUTH.

INTRODUCTION

There are two forces that control our world: The power of good and the power of evil.

The most sinister form of evil is deception. It is said in the Bible that, *"Satan masquerades as an angel of light and seeks for whom he may devour." (2 Corinthians 11:14, 1 Peter 5:8.)*

This struggle between good and evil goes back to the Garden of Eden. Just like the serpent offered Eve the forbidden fruit, we are continually bombarded with the same temptations. And that apple (or temptation) doesn't look bad. In fact, it looks shiny, red, and sweet. It appeals to our human appetite.

As we bite into it, however, our vision begins to change, and we begin to be separated from God. We are promised the knowledge of good and evil (enlightenment if you will) in exchange for the tree of life. That doesn't sound all that bad; right? I mean, everyone is searching for meaning. Apart from God's light, though, we stumble through the darkness. There lie many spiritual paths, but one is often hidden because we have an enemy that has made sure to blind our sight and a world that points in many false directions *(John 12:40)*.

Four years ago, my life drastically changed. My worldview came crashing down on me, and I was forced to face the reality of ultimate truth. I ask you, as you read these pages, can you handle the truth? And what is your basis for truth? Is it something that *feels good* to you? Perhaps, is it what you would *like to hear*? The truth God revealed to me may not provide you either. It is, however, Biblical truth.

Ever since childhood, I encountered supernatural occurrences and sought to understand these experiences. I grew up in a Christian household but preferred more esoteric forms of spirituality. I dabbled in many practices forbidden in the Bible, never grasping the danger or truly understanding who God is.

A simple prayer asking Jesus to reveal the truth began to shed light on the evil that lurked all around me. After engaging in yoga and Eastern meditation, I encountered a kundalini awakening that turned terrifying. I began searching for answers and unfolding the truth on how there is a rise of the occult and Eastern mysticism creeping into every aspect of our society. We are experiencing a paradigm shift, and even Christian churches aren't immune.

After God opened my eyes to all the deception in the occult, I began attending a New Apostolic Reformation church that was filled with New-Age practices as well. Like the New Age, Christians are looking towards an experiential faith, and God's word is slowly being changed.

We have been warned that the way to life is narrow and only a few will find it (*Matthew 7:14*). My prayer is that those who are reading this book will search for truth and do your own research. Nothing has prepared me for how narrow a path I would travel on, but I ask you to accompany me on my spiritual path to finding God's marvelous light…This is the path of finding healing, wholeness, and truth…This is the path of finding life. The path is JESUS!

Helpful Definitions

Alchemy	A seemingly magical process of transformation, creation, or combination.
Asanas	Asanas are a comfortable seated position, used to decrease restlessness during meditation.

astral travel	Leaving the physical body and travel anywhere, even throughout the universe.
Bhagavad Gita	A 700-verse Sanskrit scripture that is part of the Hindu epic Mahabharata.
Brahma	**Brahma** is the Hindu Creator god. He is also known as the Grandfather and as a later equivalent of Prajapati, the primeval first god.
Chakras	Spiritual energy centers or psychic centers. Chakras are considered physical as well as subtle and are considered the foundation of all existence, psychologically and physically.
Crystal healing	Crystal healing is a pseudoscientific alternative medicine technique that uses semiprecious stones and crystals such as quartz, amethyst or opals. Adherents of the technique claim that these have healing powers, although there is no scientific basis for this claim.
Daeva	Daeva" in Hinduism means, "The divine power itself shining and leads mankind to the Holy path by its divine light." Whereas, in Zoroastrianism, the word "deva" is derived from the root "dab," which equals, "to deceive." Daeva's are supernatural beings. In other words, they are demons.
Daeva-yasna	Daeva-yasna means "Worship of demons."

Deity	A god.
Dhyana	Meditation.
Esoteric	Intended for or likely to be understood by only a small number of people with a specialized knowledge or interest
Gnosticism	Gnosticism is a collection of ancient religious ideas and systems which originated in the first century AD among early Christian and Jewish sects. These various groups, labeled "Gnostics" by their opponents, emphasized personal spiritual knowledge over orthodox teachings, traditions, and ecclesiastical authority.
Ida	Left side of the body.
Koshas	The koshas, which are veils of energy that contain the spirit and then works through subtle bodies, which are the energy bodies that contain the human and spiritual dimensions.
Kundalini	In Hinduism, this energy is "part of a process of evolving into a union with a deity. Kundalini travels through the spine like a double helix shape, the same as how DNA works. It changes the spiritual makeup of a person. Kundalini is a process that involves the most important aspect of the human body, the spinal cord, and the nervous system: breath, organs, mind and consciousness. This

	manipulation of energy to both mind, body, and spirit is a process.
Mantras	Chant.
Nadis	Streams or conduits. nadis, which are meridian-type channels that carry energy around the body.
Pantheism	The belief that God consists of everyone and everything. For example, a tree is God, a mountain is God, the universe is God, all people are God.
Pingala	Right side of body.
Prana	Prana is achieved after the asana is conquered. Prana is thought of as the sum total of cosmic energy that is in each body.
Pranayama	The breath or control of life force energy.
Pranayama	The motion of our breath, which gains control of the prana.
Pratyahara	The withdrawal of the senses at the end of a yoga class.
Qi (pronounced chi)	The energy we manipulate, using reiki, that is thought to exist within all life forms. They also call it "prana."
Reiki	Reiki is a form of alternative medicine called energy healing. Reiki practitioners use a technique called palm healing or hands-on healing through which a "universal energy" is said to be transferred through the palms of the practitioner to the patient in order to encourage emotional or physical healing.
Samadhi (union)	Union.

Samadhi,	Peace and enlightenment.
Samayama	Concentration.
Samsara	The painful path of reincarnation.
Samyama	Infinite energy at his disposal, by the process of mortification (subduing one's bodily desires) to the body.
Sanskrit	Sanskrit is a language of ancient India with a 3,500-year history. It is the primary liturgical language of Hinduism and the predominant language of most works of Hindu philosophy as well as some of the principal texts of Buddhism and Jainism.
Seven Mountain Mandate.	The seven mountains include education, religion, family, business, government/military, arts/entertainment, and media.
Shakti	Primordial cosmic **energy** and represents the dynamic forces that are thought to move through the entire universe in Hinduism, and especially the major tradition of Hinduism, Shaktism.
Shaktipat	To initiate. Using this method, a guru can transfer his immense spiritual energy to his disciples by a mere glance or touch and completely transform them. This spiritual-energy transfer is known as "the serpent energy" or awakening of the kundalini.
Shekinah	The glory of the divine presence.
Shushma nadi	Shushma nadi is considered a central nadi that is responsible for energy that passes along the spinal cord.

Siddhas	Wise man or perfected one. Siddhas can be thought of as enlightened beings. "The siddhas are beings who are a little above ghosts. siddhas are, "Spirits in the sense of an individual or conscious spirit—of great sages from spheres of higher planes, who voluntarily incarnate in mortal bodies to help the human race in their upward progress. Siddhas are also seen as supernatural powers attained by yogis as they master the eight-fold path.
Siddhi	Magical gifts.
SOZO	Saved, healed and delivered, in Greek
Syncretism	The amalgamation or attempted amalgamation of different religions, cultures, or schools of thought.
The Christ spirit	Lucifer, the light bringer.
The Yoga Sutras of Patanjali	A collection of 196 Indian sutras on the theory and practice of yoga. The Yoga Sutras were compiled prior to 400 CE by Patanjali who synthesized and organized knowledge about yoga from older traditions.
Yasna	Yasna literally means "oblation" or "worship."
Yoga	To yoke. A Hindu theistic philosophy teaching suppression of all activity of the mind, body, and will in order that the self may realize its distinction from them and attain liberation.
Yogi	A Yoga master.

PART I

SEEDS OF DECEPTION

Chapter 1

Darkness Beckons

I'm wide awake. It's the middle of the night, and the only thing my eyes can focus on is the pitch black as I struggle for my vision to adjust. Fear grips me as I realize I'm alone. I pull the blankets closer around my neck. Before I can cry out to my parents, my gaze turns towards the hallway, and I become frozen with awe. There, standing at the end of the hallway, I see an apparition of a woman. Her hair is up in a bun, she is wearing a glowing, white dress, and her body is translucent. She has beady black eyes that zero in on me and pierce right through my young soul. This female being starts to effortlessly glide across the floor and head straight to my room. My awe instantly turns to terror as I throw the blankets over my head and refuse to move until morning.

This scene would become one of my earliest memories. I must have been about five or six years old but would remember that image vividly for the rest of my life. In that moment, my life was being shaped and my curiosity piqued. The apparition seemed to appear to me with a mission in mind, and it wouldn't be the last time paranormal events would plague my childhood.

At the age of six, I had no idea what it was that I had witnessed. Most would have described it as a "ghost"; however, at my age I didn't even have that word in my vocabulary. I remember on a couple of occasions trying to explain to my mom that I had seen something, but I was lacking an appropriate way to express my thoughts, often causing her to brush me off.

It wouldn't be until several years later, when I started watching paranormal shows on TV, that I told her that I had seen a so-called "ghost." Ever since then, I would always sleep with my door closed, afraid of what I'd encounter in the middle of the night. Throughout much of my childhood, many strange things happened to me when I was alone. I would go to sleep at night with the sense of an eerie presence watching me. Other times I'd be startled awake, hearing someone screaming my name in my ear, but no one was there. Often, I would be haunted by terrifying nightmares, even vivid apocalyptic dreams I can still remember today.

I remember one dream; it was of pure chaos. I saw people running all over the place, while the streets were filled with violence and bloodshed. There were huge fountains outside that were filling with blood, and people were wearing black, hooded gowns. Next to one fountain was a young girl with blonde hair and mesmerizingly big, blue eyes. I remember her standing still amongst the chaos and staring at me. Then my dream would end.

I never understood these dreams or why I've always remembered them. All I know is my interest in the supernatural was forming. I had seen and felt too much and knew there was more to this world than meets the eye.

My family had moved to Connecticut when I was five years old. Prior to that, my parents were married then divorced. At the time, my father had problems with his drinking, causing my mom to separate from him. After my mom left him, he wanted his family back. He walked back into our lives and convinced my mom he was different now: He had found Jesus.

It was after my parents got back together that we moved to Connecticut, where my dad was from. After living with my grandmother for a while, we bought a small home. This would be the home I grew up in and the home I would encounter strange events, that would appear to target only me.

I grew up in a Christian household, my mother a Catholic and my dad a born-again Christian. My family would often bring me and my younger sister to church, but I never understood who

Jesus was. I only understood it was our religion. I never put much thought into Christianity, I was too busy trying to make sense of the supernatural world I felt around me.

Deep down inside I was always searching for answers, and church didn't do it for me. As an adolescent and teen, I became obsessed with the paranormal and the occult. The word "occult" means hidden, or secret. Well, I knew there was a hidden world, and it fascinated me!

I spent hours reading and researching all things paranormal. I even wanted to visit any haunted areas I could. I was drawn to psychics and astrology. I loved gaining esoteric knowledge and thought I possessed some psychic abilities myself. I often knew things would happen before they did, and I could walk into a house and know that spirits inhabited that house.

I became enchanted with the hidden world around me, and I couldn't get enough. At one point, I wanted to become an astrologer and parapsychologist. I delved into the subject of astrology and learned how to write up whole birth charts. I was good at it and believed it to be true. I would hear that psychics or astrology was evil but thought that thinking was narrowminded. God created the stars and planets, how could reading them be evil? Most psychics I knew seemed to help people, so it made perfect sense that God would give people certain gifts.

You see, I believed in God, but I considered myself deeply spiritual, never *religious*.

The more I delved into these subjects, the more I began to fear going to sleep at night. I would often feel an oppressive presence around me, and I started to experience bouts of depression. There were times I would sit in my room, and I couldn't stop crying. At one point, I remember falling asleep and having a terrifying nightmare. In my dream, I was in my house and running from this female spirit. This was the same spirit I had seen when I was a child, only now her face was demonic. I remember her grabbing me viciously by the throat and throwing me into the wall, hard. This may have only been a nightmare, but I *felt* the pain, and the force of being thrown woke me up

I would lie in bed terrified, with my heart beating so hard I thought it might beat right out of my chest. I couldn't forget the look of sheer hatred on that demonic spirit's face. This was *not* only a dream.

My sister would tell me anytime I was away from the house, she would sleep in my bedroom, and she too would encounter nightmares. My mother also reported that she had heard footsteps down the stairs at night. My involvement with the occult was opening doors in my life, but I couldn't see the connection at the time. However, I would attend church on Sundays and go to youth group.

One friend I had made was a guy around my age named Jesse. He differed greatly from me. He was religious and had been "born again" since he was a young child. I was rebellious and considered myself to be spiritual, not religious like he was. He would often talk to me about God and extend an invitation to several youth events. I thought he was a little weird, but his friendship started to grow on me. Come to think of it, I suppose God was already calling me to follow Him through the voice of this church friend.

I remained friends with this kid through most of my teen years. He would often call me at home, and we would talk for hours. He always seemed to call me at the most opportune times: times I was battling depression or when I had no one else to talk to. I found it peculiar he would pursue me for friendship. Here I was, a broken, rebellious teen; someone who drank at 14; and someone who would sneak out at night, hang out with the wrong people, then get dragged to church Sunday morning, hung over.

This was my first lesson on who God was. Although I was on a path to destruction, He was trying to reach me through my friend at church. If I was feeling hopeless or alone, crying, I could count on Jesse calling me and speaking life into my despair.

Jesse would often talk to me about his faith and his spiritual experiences with God and demons. I found these conversations interesting and had my own spiritual experiences to share. I explained to him my intense interest in the paranormal and my first time seeing an apparition. His response would embed in my memory forever.

He stated, *"That ghost you saw as a child was not a ghost. It was a demon, and that demon was planting a seed, a seed of interest so you would follow the things of darkness."*

His terrifying words sent chills up my spine. I became indignant at that response and denied it—although I never could erase his words from my mind. It's amazing the small details one will remember in their lifetime. Jesse's words became seared into my spirit, and I did not understand how prophetic those words would become. If only I could see God's future for me, then His words would make sense, and I would understand the real battle between Good and evil.

God knows the plans He has for you. One to give you a future. One of hope and not of harm *(Jeremiah 29:11)*. But the enemy comes only to kill, steal and destroy *(John 10: 8-10)*.

Whatever sensitivity I had to the things of the spirit world, the devil wanted to use for his own cause. He wanted to destroy my calling and who I was in Christ. The enemy was destroying me and leading me away from God and His truth, which is only found in Jesus.

I continued down a path of a New Age spirituality, consulting psychics, reading tarot cards, and searching for all things mystical. My depression often became crippling, and I would experience a great emptiness inside. At one point, I became so scared to sleep alone in my room that I found a Jesus picture and prayer hanging inside my mom's bedroom. I didn't understand who this Jesus guy was, but I took it out of my mother's room and hung it in the corner of my bedroom.

That night I said the prayer out loud and begged for God's help. I wanted to feel peace, and that prayer worked! For weeks afterward I felt the atmosphere in my room had changed. I could sleep at peace again. This would be my first encounter with Jesus that showed a sense of His power and presence. There was a power in His name I didn't understand.

CHAPTER 2
SEDUCTION

I've always been an inquisitive and curious person. As a child, I loved gaining knowledge and had a thirst for the unknown. My favorite place to be was the bookstore. I would comb the shelves, searching for mystery and intrigue. The New Age Section would keep me busy for hours. I would buy books about hauntings, angel encounters, and astrology books of every kind. Astrology was my favorite; there was so much to learn! I remember taking up intense study on how to complete whole birth charts on people. It was so fascinating how the planetary alignments would lay out a blueprint of a person's life. Often, upon meeting someone, I could tell right away what sign they were. When using someone's chart to read them, I felt it gave me insight to what God had already destined someone to become.

Along with this propensity toward the paranormal, at an early age I discovered a love for writing. English was my favorite subject, and, when given assignments, I would get lost in my imagination. It was also a wonderful way to express myself, and I came to enjoy poetry. I liked the dark side of stuff and loved reading Edgar Allan Poe and horror books and movies. I have since realized that every gift or talent I had was used to serve the enemy. My poetry was dark, and though I was sensitive to the supernatural, that sensitivity led me on a path to the occult and mysticism. I knew there was more than the natural world, and I always craved a way to connect to the ethereal. Deep down inside, I wanted to connect to God, but the enemy wanted to pervert that and prevent me from ever connecting to the God of the Bible.

The pull I felt to explore the occult was almost like being under a spell. It consumed me. It blinded me to truth and offered me a sensual, carnal wisdom that was earthly, not at all from above (*James 3:15*). I pursued what I thought was divine or unknown in every place except for one: The Bible. Instead, I sought answers from psychics, palm readings, and was fascinated by watching mediums on popular TV shows. They appeared to be such good people that were helping others find answers, even help solve crimes; surely these people had God-given gifts.

* * *

I remember my first time going to a psychic fair. The atmosphere was so inviting, and the vendors exuded such charm. The entire fair appeals to your senses. The smell of incense and essential oils; the colorful, trance-like artwork and beautiful crystals; hearing healing music and introductions to the newest holistic healing modalities.

The place was filled with psychic mediums and every type of enchantment and form of divination imaginable. That day I would go to two psychics who both had a hard time reading me.

However, I met an astrologer there who said many true things to me: it was the confirmation of why I loved astrology. I even viewed it as a science. I had plans to go to a college for astrology. Being a spiritual person, my beliefs would always intertwine with my life plans. It's who I was.

The mystical always lured me in. Jesus was always in the back of mind and my parents were Christians, but they were ignorant to Satan's devices.

It never even occurred to me that maybe the source of information psychics and mediums were receiving was not from God. People want to connect with dead loved ones, but God strictly forbids this in His word:

- *(Isaiah 47:13)* You are wearied with your many counsels; let now the astrologers, those who prophesy by the stars, those who predict by the new moon, stand up and save you from what will come upon you.

- *(Leviticus 20:6)* As for the person who turns to mediums and to spiritists, to play the harlot after them, I will set my face against that person and will cut him off from among his people.

- *(Leviticus 19:31)* Do not turn to mediums or spiritists; do not seek them out to be defiled by them. I AM the LORD your God.

- *(Deuteronomy 18:10)* There shall not be found among you anyone who makes his son or his daughter pass through the fire, one who uses divination, one who practices witchcraft, or one who interprets omens, or a sorcerer.

- *(Isaiah 8:19)* When they say to you, "Consult the mediums and the spiritists who whisper and mutter," should not a people consult their God? Should they consult the dead on behalf of the living?

If one believes in the supernatural, then one must believe that there are evil spirits in that plane. How could we, with our limited human understanding, think we couldn't be deceived? Cosmic powers hold the upper hand; they are a realm we cannot see, and therefore we mustn't seek the supernatural. God forbids this for our own safety. As we just saw, God has made this very clear in scripture.

The occult, divination, and spiritualism are concepts that go back to the beginning of time. They are methods of seeking answers apart from God. It is distrust in the Word of God and opens doors to your life that may not be easy to close.

I gave the devil a foothold in my life for many years. I was a rebellious teen and started drinking at age fourteen. I was selfish and had a very skewed view of what a "good person" was.

I believed in God but considered myself "spiritual." To me "religious" people were brainwashed. Experiencing the supernatural as a kid left me with questions, and I was trying to make sense of the paranormal. I would read about local hauntings and want to go to these places. It fascinated me. I was very sensitive to this realm my whole life. Often, I could walk into a house or place and sense different presences. Anything I tried to do to become a psychic or acquire intuitive abilities would develop quickly, but that would lead to experiences that scared me. I never listened to the quiet voice within me that was warning me.

After I graduated high school, I moved out of my parents' house because I had a rocky relationship with my mother. It was during this time that I moved in with my best friend and started experimenting with drugs. We would party every weekend, using ecstasy, mushrooms and sometimes cocaine. I loved the escape from reality, but this was the darkest time in my life. I cared about little else but getting high for two years and was reckless and out of control. Looking back, it's a true miracle that I am even alive. I believe using drugs is another way to open your consciousness to dark powers. Again, this gave the enemy of our souls a way to destroy our minds and spirit. Me and my friend split ways. Our friendship fell apart, and I moved out.

I moved in with an older woman that lived in the neighborhood I grew up in. She let me rent a room for free for helping her do odd jobs. This woman was into New Age things and was very intuitive. She was interested in casting spells and had a special deck of tarot cards she would use and read on me. I remember her telling me that a certain deck gets used to the person who owns them, and it's important not to do readings on people from someone else's deck. So, I purchased my own. I would study reading them every day. It was easy to connect with them and pick up messages when laying the cards out. However, I lost interest in card readings because, when I would go to sleep at night, I would feel an eerie presence watching me and would get woken up to the sound of clawing on the walls. I decided that card reading was too dark, although I toyed with the idea of perhaps angel cards because it appeared more positive to receive messages from angels. Nonetheless, something stopped my interest in those readings.

Although I questioned if there was a true God, He never stopped looking out for me. I would often come across Godly people during this time. I remember being at work one day and one of my clients stops me while walking by and says, "You know, God loves you a lot!"

There was a sparkle in her eyes I will never forget. She exuded such a light about her, and her words touched me. Deep down inside, I believed her. I mean, I was raised as a Christian and adored Christ, but I never knew Him and preferred following my path, even if my path was one of destruction.

I didn't know the Bible, and I didn't believe the Bible was the infallible book of God. Who could be that naïve? It was clearly a book written by man. But God always has plans, and sometimes He will let us fall so far down that He will be the only one able to catch us.

I suffered many bouts of depression throughout the years, but, after I became pregnant with my first son, my life seemed to come crashing down. The increasing hormones of pregnancy started to wreak havoc on my brain. For the first time, I experienced very unstable mood swings and panic attacks that would come out of the blue. When my son was born, I was so in love and wanted to change my life around. I no longer wanted to do drugs or act wild. I wanted to live my life for my son and try to be the best mom I could be.

It was the day he was born that my then live-in boyfriend would propose to me. I loved this new start to life! However, about a year later, I became an absolute mess. I had reached such a dark time in my life, one that made me almost lose my entire will to live. I started to come apart at the seams and felt like I was losing my soul. As I watched my child grow, memories flooded my psyche; ones I had disassociated myself from; dark, repressed memories I had convinced myself never happened. Now, I was being reminded and tormented.

When I was young, a babysitter molested me, and I could vividly remember the details. I had never told anyone before, and now my anxiety was getting out of control. I developed severe insomnia along with depression so bad that it hurt to get out of bed. I became angry and a very impatient, distant parent.

Although I did pray to God for help, I also consulted psychics and still held to my New Age beliefs. I felt like I was losing control of my life, and I wanted to die. I would even come up with plans to harm myself. Every time I looked in the mirror, I hated the person looking back at me. The darkness was consuming me, and I was trying very hard to appear normal to the outside world.

I knew I needed to get help, and I remember praying to God about it. Finally, I was able to get health insurance, and this was a blessing because now I could seek help for my condition. I saw a therapist who suggested trying an antidepressant. The antidepressant the doctor put me on was an absolute miracle drug. Within weeks I could sleep again, my mood started to lift, and all anxiety attacks stopped. It felt so good to breathe again. I no longer yelled at my son, and I felt like I had the energy to take on the tasks of daily life. I guess the only thought in my head at the time was, would my life depend on a drug? This became a scary thought to me; one I didn't want to think about at the time. I was happy, and I needed happy right then.

I felt very lucky that the first medication I tried worked for me because I knew some never found the right drug. I hated that thought of others suffering. If I had never suffered this ordeal, there would be no way possible for me to understand the horror of mental illness. It was something no medical professional could explain. Our mind and spirits are intertwined, and often that spiritual aspect is neglected. Because of what I had gone through, I wanted to help others who were suffering. I wanted to reach people and try to lead them to a light in the darkness. Even though I didn't yet know *who* that light in the darkness would be.

At this point I was ready to change my career: I wanted to go into mental health.

CHAPTER 3
NEW AGE-OLD LIES

Juggling the school/family life balance was a challenge, and one day when I arrived home from school, I chose to sit in my car for a few minutes before going inside to be a mom. I was starting to think about my future, and I had big plans for my life. I wanted my kids to see me succeed.

I got out of my car and headed for my mailbox. As I reached in, I pulled out an envelope from a nursing school I applied to. My heart sank a little. Oh, great, I thought, it's a rejection letter! Nursing school was so competitive, and I applied last minute, so I wasn't feeling optimistic.

I ran inside and ripped open the top. As I pulled out the letter, my mouth dropped. The words at the top read: "Dear Tara, we are excited to tell you, we have selected you for our program in the Fall."

I couldn't believe it! I had been working hard in school for the last two years, while having four kids, one of which was a newborn. "God heard my prayers," I whispered to myself.

This one letter meant my entire life was about to change, and it filled me with such gratitude. I knew right away my focus would be mental health nursing, and I thanked God for this opportunity. I knew, firsthand, the complete anguish of anxiety and depression, and I couldn't wait to help others. I used to tell myself that I would never let my pain be in vain. I had enough wisdom to know that all suffering had meaning. Whatever we go through in life can always launch us forward in helping others.

I sat there thinking about all the holistic ways I could help. I was learning about so many natural methods: herbs; nutrition; chakras; acupuncture; and, my favorite, yoga! Yoga was so peaceful, so calming.

Yoga made me feel connected to God and would ease my stress. It was all about strengthening body, mind, and spirit. I even noticed there was a lot of yoga nurses, and I had plans to become a certified yoga instructor and reiki master. I loved how all this was coming together. In fact, I felt in my heart that God was leading my steps. Little did I know how much *He was* leading my steps and that my world would later be flipped upside down.

I was approaching a pivotal point in my life and started to be concerned with what my belief system was. I was raised Christian but started wondering if that was what I believed, or was it only what someone taught me? As a person who searched for truth, I was ready to dig deeper. I took a world religion class in college and began to deepen my understanding of what other religions believed. There were many similarities between different religions, and I fell in love with Buddhism and Hinduism.

These religions seemed like more of a way of life and much less dogmatic than the Abrahamic religions. They taught love, peace, and mysticism. It felt right to me. I loved the wisdom they espoused. However, I still wanted to cling to the Jesus I grew up with.

At this point in my life, I was immersed in my yoga practice and meditation. I saw no wrong in incorporating Jesus into these mystical practices. As I studied Eastern Orthodox Christianity and Gnosticism, I could see real parallels with the practices in Eastern mysticism. I began a quest for truth, and I was determined to find it. One quote that began to resonate with me during this time was a quote by the mystic, Rumi: "What you are seeking is also seeking you."

How true, I thought! I was on a mystical journey, one that would turn out very different from what I could have ever imagined.

* * *

My oldest son confided in me that he too had seen apparitions since childhood. One day he described to me what looked like heat waves surrounding people and would even see slight color around them. Was he seeing auras? I was very curious and searched metaphysical websites and groups. Sure enough, people that could see auras described it like he had stated. I must admit, I became excited. My son was gifted! I now see this as a distraction because I would spend hours every day engaging with these psychic groups. It sucked me in.

During this time, I deepened my meditation practice. Life was always so busy, it was a way for me to slow down, focus, and concentrate on my breathing. In these moments, I tried to quiet my mind and fade from reality. I was getting better at emptying my thoughts. However, in these moments, I would often feel an eerie presence surround me. No matter. I would shrug it off and continue on my path.

As I engaged with people exploring the metaphysical, one thing I noticed was how many would also experience paranormal events in their home or spoke with spirit guides. I felt uneasy in my home and started to wonder if these things opened doors to one's life.

A turning point for me was the night my son frantically called me over to the top of our stairs: "Mom, something dark just ran by; it was darker than night!"

I rushed him to his room and explained to him that nothing was there, but, inside myself, I knew he was telling the truth. I wasn't sleeping well and would hear strange sounds in my room at night. Whenever I would take pictures in my home, I would find orbs in them. I came across different testimonials from ex-psychics and mediums that had encountered Jesus. They often told of how their once-friendly spirit guides now turned dark and angry.

This opened my eyes to realize a spirit realm we have no control over. It was shocking at that point to understand that demons can, and often do, masquerade as something beautiful, often helpful, to take your focus off serving the one true God. I got to a place where I could understand psychic/medium deception, but when I stumbled upon a video calling yoga demonic, it outraged me!

Now, this is why Christians embarrass me, I thought. Yoga is exercise, and it gives me peace. That's what it boiled down to. If it made me feel good, then that's all that mattered. I had so many excuses. If someone had a bad experience with yoga, that was just them. Perhaps they were doing too much yoga or making it too spiritual. It gave me peace of mind, stretched out my body, and I could easily connect with *my* God while doing so. It was a practice I could make my own. Besides, only connecting to the Bible was narrowminded; God was much too big to be kept in a box!

In New Age, life was about experiences, feelings, and discovering your inner truth. People often talked of losing the "ego," but we're only becoming more egotistical than ever. The yoga path of spirituality was leading you inward; everything you wanted could be accessed by searching within; it was a religion that could be summed up as "selfism."

It had little to do with sacrifice, instead the practices were about puffing you up with pride and becoming the divine spark within. Who would need to look outward to a God when you could become your own god? You could heal yourself, and even learn how to speak things into existence, such as the law of attraction. It was all about *me*! Why should I suffer or care about sin? I could do good deeds and access the universe by going within. What need would I have for a wrathful God?

Soon, all my beliefs left me with was my own experiences and a superficial love for others. I wrapped all of this in an ideal of love, light, and unity.

* * *

By the time I was twenty-six, I began leaving certain practices behind. I was no longer interested in clairvoyance or tarot cards. Now I looked for holistic healing methods: practices I found healing to the body and soul.

Yoga became my place of rest. I could make it my own beautiful practice. Whatever stress I was facing, I could leave it at the door when I entered any yoga studio. Yoga allowed me a chance to breath and expand my lungs with oxygen that all my cells would need. As my breath would align with every posture, deeper I would move into each asana. During my practice, each breath, movement, and meditation combined to create a unique formulation for a mind and body release. As my movement grew stronger, my mental focus and clarity increased. At the end of class, we would finish with aroma therapy, the gentle vibration from singing bowls, and a relaxing meditation to free my thoughts. I would leave refreshed and renewed, ready to dig further into my studies. I loved Jesus, but He wasn't the forefront of my life. I didn't rely on Him for *His* rest, I found it elsewhere.

As I worked my way through nursing school, I saw so much need for the help that yoga, as well as reiki, could bring. In hospitals, they usually called energy work "therapeutic touch." In certain studies, it was shown to ease pain, nausea, and often could help one feel more relaxed. I wanted to help people, and this seemed like an amazing opportunity to do so.

Both yoga and reiki work off a universal life force energy. Qi (pronounced chi) is the energy we manipulate, using reiki, that is thought to exist within all life forms. They also call it "prana" when being spoken of by yoga practitioners. It is a flow of universal energy that connects mind and body. By a practice of yoga and meditation, one could become a conduit for healing energy.

On the surface, this appeared beautiful and natural. It was fascinating what our own body and minds could accomplish. Yoga worked together like a divine system, often called "the eight limbs of yoga." Most important during yoga was asanas, which are the postures. Pranayama was the breath or control of life force energy. Pratyahara is the withdrawal of the senses, and at the end of class, Dhyana or meditation. With these combined, one could attain "samadhi," or peace and enlightenment.

Yoga is taught as an exercise, with its spiritual roots often ignored. Yoga is a form of spirituality and because there's no dogma attached; it appears compatible with any religion. For me that was the case; I was "spiritual" and thought this was a neutral system I could combine with Christianity. What started as an exercise for me became a place of inner peace and an idol I would look to, to enable healing of body and spirit. What I didn't understand at the time was, I was following a path outside of Jesus and one outside of God's will. I was a "Christian" by religious title only. I didn't know God. I was always looking elsewhere to fulfill what only *He* could provide. I would continue in my yoga practice and study things such as chakras, crystal healing, and reiki healing energy.

During this time, I had made a friend I looked up to. She was my yoga instructor and was a reiki practitioner. I admired her: her love, her warmth, and her knowledge. The love and light of the New Age crowd drew me in. I often found them to be so much more inviting than any Christian I had ever met.

My yoga friend taught yoga training classes and reiki. This would be perfect, I thought. In a weekend, I could get yoga certified and learn reiki. I was so excited as I looked over the itinerary for the certification. When looking at a yoga teacher training syllabus, I found that we had to study the Bhagavad Gita as part of the training. I began to question this. I'm not sure why, but this course of study bothered me. Why do I need to study a religious text to teach "exercise"? Perhaps there was more darkness to Yoga than I was previously willing to admit.

I had reached a point in my life where I wanted to follow Jesus; I wasn't sure who He was, and studying the Bhagavad Gita sent questions spiraling through my head. I prayed to God and asked Him if becoming a yoga instructor and a reiki master was something He would approve of. I explained to God that I wanted to help people. Could He please show me the truth? I wanted to be on the right path and hoped that the God of the universe agreed with my choices.

PART II

SEEKING FOR TRUTH

CHAPTER 4
A STILL SMALL VOICE

After the birth of my fourth son, it was common for me to have difficulty sleeping. Some nights were incredibly hard to fall asleep. I suffered from insomnia; my mind constantly active. Stretching and meditation before bedtime was starting to help. I had intensified my yoga practice and was attending more classes now. It became a daily habit to pray to God, while utilizing yoga and meditation as a means for connecting to Him. I tried to read the Bible a few times and couldn't seem to understand it at all. Overwhelmed, I began to feel a sense of dissatisfaction to my soul. There was a void, and I was trying to fill it with whatever spirituality felt good.

Somehow, during this time, I stumbled on a book called "*The Beautiful Side of Evil*," by Johanna Michaelson. I was shocked at the title. Could evil really be beautiful? We are taught that evil equals bad, ugly, and something that feels wrong. I was learning; however, the greatest evil comes in the form of deception.

In "*The Beautiful Side of Evil*," Johanna tells her story of encountering supernatural spirits since childhood (something I could already relate to). She grew up sensitive to the spirit realm and later would encounter a spiritual healer named Pichita, in Mexico.

Pichita was a medium-type healer, who would let a benevolent spirit enter her body and perform psychic surgery. People would come from all the world to seek out her out, believing that her healing power was from "God." Johanna would come to believe that her gifts were special, and she began working for this healer.

Johanna would often see crosses hanging on the wall and witness thanks and praise given to Jesus. She truly believed she was doing God's work. Johanna experienced out-of-body experiences and mind control. She even thought her spirit guide was Jesus because that's how he appeared to her, only to reveal himself as something hideous looking at another point.

Johanna, despite being warned about it by a Christian couple she ended up staying with, also engaged in yoga. Her book was thought provoking and opened my eyes to a reality I never imagined before. On the back cover of "*The Beautiful Side of Evil,*" a question stops me in my tracks: *"Are all miracles from God, or is there a beautiful side of evil? The blind see, the deaf hear, and the lame walk. Is God always behind such miracles, or can there be another source?"*

In her eye-opening search for truth, Johanna finds the true Jesus of the Bible, only to face full-on demonic attack. I had found this book, miraculously, at exactly the right time. I started to question everything, and this would be the beginning of the veil of deception being lifted from my eyes.

Although this was opening doors for the Holy Spirit to work in my life, I would still hold on to my yoga practice. I still made excuses as to why this was okay. After all, it was producing some positive effects in my life, and perhaps people who had bad experiences were too into the Hinduism aspect of the practice. Not me. I was using it to glorify God. I could take this practice and offer praise and prayer. Using this methodology, I could make it my own.

Again, things became about *me*, and I wanted to worship God without giving a single thought as to what was acceptable in God's eyes. What I was about to find out was how we worship God, and what we believe about Him, says everything about our relationship with Him. Jesus himself asked the question: "Who do you say that I am?" That was a very important question. Truth is a black and white issue.

In the New Age, everyone believed in their own truth. What was true to one, wasn't necessarily someone else's truth. And that was okay because truth was subjective. So, what exactly was the truth, I wondered? The only constant in life was death; it is our only guarantee. When we each reach that fateful day, will our "own" truth play out? Probably not. What is real truth, God's undeniable truth, will happen whether we believed it now or not.

I started going to a couple different yoga studios, and one was very spiritual. One of the yoga teachers was a kundalini yoga teacher, and the atmosphere was great! What is kundalini? Kundalini is very important in Hinduism. It is thought of as a serpent energy that lies dormant at the base of one's spine. As it awakens, it springs upward through your spine, reaching all the chakras (energy centers) until it reaches your crown chakra.

Everyone in this class was so warm and loving. It was a sacred space to me, and one that filled me with peace. I would often leave yoga class feeling totally refreshed and renewed. On many other occasions, however, a day or two later, I would feel unusually emotional or even super angry. I couldn't understand why. I mean, I'd found peace; however, the peace that yoga would give me was temporary and fleeting. It never seemed to last. Many nights I would drift to sleep and be awakened by feeling like my spirit was floating. I felt I could start to project right out of my body and would immediately wake up because the loss of control would frighten me. There was this heaviness on my chest, and as I tried to move, I felt held down.

Now, I struggled with nightmares my entire life, but what I was experiencing was sleep paralysis. This had never happened to me before, and, luckily, I was able to quickly come out of this paralyzed dream state. Sleep paralysis is something I learned about in college, but why was it happening to me? I felt my body and mind were beginning to change.

According to Shiel (2018), *"Sleep paralysis is a frightening form of paralysis that occurs when a person suddenly finds himself or herself unable to move for a few minutes, often upon falling asleep or waking up... The symptoms of sleep paralysis include sensations of noises, smells, levitation, terror, and images of frightening intruders."*

In many cultures around the world and in the Christian worldview, this is a demonic-type attack. My dreams were becoming more lucid, and sleep would be difficult because, as my eyes would close, I noticed I could begin to see around the room as if my eyes were still open. I was developing a different type of sight. It was incredible. I thought I was growing spiritually and intuitively. Learning about chakras and manipulating the energy within my body had made any psychic phenomena seem almost natural: a hidden part of our consciousness that could be awakened. I loved this idea. In Eastern religions this could be seen as opening your third eye. This was an invisible, esoteric, psychic perception that could be awakened through yoga and meditation practices.

I was learning about Astral travel and how one could leave their own body and travel anywhere, even throughout the universe. I believed, in a way, my body and spirit were getting ready for this type of adventure. At the same time, this prospect scared me a bit. I had read a few accounts of people who engaged in astral traveling, and, while they stared down at their sleeping bodies, they would also see demonic or hooded-type figures surrounding them. Could something enter a body while your spirit was absent? Every time I would start to embrace some New Age teaching, somehow, God would place a source of truth in my path that would stop me in my tracks.

As much as I tried to delve into the mystical, I always felt a slight tug on my spirit that something more sinister lay beneath. But I ignored that quiet voice, while being seduced onto the wrong path. There was a veil of deceit that clouded my vision. My prayers were about to be answered, though, and my life shaken upside down. I had taken a step to really let go and try to be free in yoga practice. I was ready to worship God and take a mystical approach to encountering the Holy Spirit. I had been suffering from postpartum depression, like many times before, but now the antidepressants had started to worsen my condition. I had stopped taking them but could not seem to feel like myself. I felt forever changed by this medication.

What could possibly be my answer now?

I needed a miracle. I was on my way to a restorative yoga class. My mind, soul, and body desperately needed rest. I entered the studio with a sense of relief and a willingness to let go. As I sat down in a comfortable position, I took note of my surroundings and tried to breath and be in the moment.

This day felt different to me. Things were about to change. I could feel it in my spirit. I took a deep, cleansing breath in, and then exhaled all my stress. From asana to asana, I would effortlessly move. I would hold these positions longer than usual, and my mental control was amazingly strong tonight. As I meditated throughout these positions, I could feel a release in my soul. Tonight, more than ever, there was something beautiful and enchanting around me. As I moved from downward-facing dog to child's pose, I would gently whisper for "Holy Spirit."

As I sat there in deep meditation and praying for God's presence, something amazing happened. I felt like I was fading from existence, my thoughts erased. Suddenly I could see the most amazing colors and warmth emanating from my entire being. During meditation, I could now see the most intense magenta color with my spirit. I felt a warm embrace. Finally, I had found peace, beautiful peace.

As I drove home that night, I felt an immense amount of gratitude. At last, my mind felt so sharp, so clear. Come to think of it, I felt almost like I had a high. Wow! I felt amazing. My life, my thoughts, my mind were all changing. I didn't know what was happening to me, but all of it felt so right. I'd found the answers to my problems. I felt excited. This was my answer: spiritual awakening.

I now knew I needed to deepen my practice and do it more often, perhaps even daily. I became obsessed and, slowly, I would be more and more led away with this practice. It became my new spirituality. Jesus of the Bible would become a distant memory because I had replaced Him with a Jesus of my own making.

As the days went on, I felt such a strong urge to do yoga. I was ready to deepen my practice, and I came to the realization that yoga was the answer. After leaving class one day, I noticed something within me was starting to change. I began to look at things differently and felt so compassionate towards others. My heart was softening, and I felt like I had embraced a divine spark: a universal light that is in us all. I was adopting a view of universalism and embracing a New Age mindset, a smorgasbord of spiritual delights for my own choosing.

I had a very spiritual, not dogmatic, view of God. I enjoyed trying to have some sort of mystical union with Jesus. Yoga was perfect for this. Yoga means to "yoke," to become one with Brahma. Yoga is a spiritual system, one that will open your chakras (spiritual energy centers), and align your body, mind, and spirit while eventually leading to enlightenment and end the cycles of reincarnation. "Enlightenment," essentially, is a form of death. I will discuss this more in another chapter.

The more I prayed, the more I began to feel spiritually altered at a rapid pace. I had always been sensitive to the spirit realm, and anything I dabbled in would encapsulate me quickly. Whenever I would practice yoga, I could feel these electrifying energy surges shooting throughout my body. It was these same energy surges within my body that would help propel me into deeper yoga postures, and I started to feel amazing strength. The breath, the movement, and concentration of my mind were beautifully starting to blend.

Often, coming home from school, I would feel strong urges to break out into yoga poses and would find myself almost needing to in order to release this energy I had going through me. At times I would even feel strangely sexually aroused. I will admit some of this started to feel a bit overpowering. I began further questioning and praying for answers. I only wanted the truth and was willing to hear answers that maybe I didn't want to hear.

CHAPTER 5
EYES TO SEE

(John 12:40)
He has blinded their eyes and hardened their hearts,
lest they should see with their eyes, lest they should understand
with their hearts and turn, so that I should heal them.

At this point in my life, I was about 34, halfway through nursing school, and depression was creeping back into my life; my anxiety was at an all-time high. I again suffered from postpartum depression, coupled with lack of sleep, and I was trying to make it to graduation. Some days I was filled with frustration and sorrow.

I had tried several natural healing modalities and every New Age practice I could think of. I went back on a low-dose antidepressant, thinking it would get me by, but this time was different. This time I wasn't able to sleep, and, for the first time, I found myself more suicidal than ever. I found it painful to climb out of bed in the morning and would often cry myself to sleep. I felt tormented. I hated myself. This drug that had worked miracles for me before was now worsening my symptoms. I stopped taking it and felt better. I was still sad but at least not borderline psychotic.

I did not understand what to do anymore. What did my life now hold? As I lay in bed at night, not only could I see around the room with my eyes shut, but I began having full-on, vivid visions. These were not hallucinations. I would close my eyes, and it was

29

like looking at a superimposed movie screen. I would see people and events, wars even. Soon the visions became frightening, and I began being scared to go to sleep at night. I had always suffered with nightmares, since childhood, but had never had strange visions before. Things were getting bizarre and frightening.

The frightening visions and being able to see around the room with my eyes shut were signs of kundalini spiritual awakening. However, I barely knew who I was anymore and felt so empty. I was trying so hard to keep it all together. I was a mom, a wife, and now I was barely hanging on by a thread in school. Fatigue overwhelmed me; I was tired of trying and ready to let go. There were times I begged death to take me. I was desperate for the peace I would gain from eternal rest.

The only thing that kept me hanging on was my Christian upbringing and the threat of hell for committing suicide. But I already felt like my soul had died. I was a shell of a person, and the more I did yoga and prayed, the worse I would feel. "What was happening?" I cried to God. "Please end this suffering, Lord."

I don't even think I knew what happiness felt like at this point. I even felt like my soul was separating from my physical body. There were moments I would walk down a hallway and feel disoriented and as if I was growing larger or taller. It frightened me because I couldn't seem to make sense of what I was going through. Was this what "becoming one with the universe" was? I felt like a drop of water falling into the ocean, becoming part of the whole, and losing my individuality.

I would comb through yoga and higher consciousness forums, reading people's experiences about evolving into a higher consciousness. I would often see posts where people would have strange meditation (almost hallucinations) while meditating. Enthusiasts would speak of kundalini energy that lay dormant, like a serpent, at the base of the spine. Awakening this energy was often the goal of yoga. Yoga was popular exercise in the US, but this practice was far away from simply "exercise." It started to seem like a mass effort to alter people's consciousness.

The more I prayed; the more things began to look different to me. Everything I learned was love, light, and acceptance. Nothing was ever questioned. Why was yoga/meditation gaining popularity so quickly? Well, it benefited every area of the being that you could think of. I started to see a rise to teach it everywhere: schools for our children and even in the medical field. There was so much more to this ancient practice. Why did everyone think it was so innocent? I was finding out that yoga is, and always will be, Hinduism. Why were Eastern practices being introduced into every aspect of life? I started to believe I was opening myself up to the spiritual realm and was awakening this serpent spirit within me.

A turning point happened one night as I lay down my head to sleep. As soon as my body started to relax and I closed my eyes, the most horrifying vision appeared to me. There was a huge demonic face staring down at me. This was a vivid impression, and it was no dream. I felt as if I was peering into the spirit realm, and I was seeing what was there. It was a real-life spiritual monster, with glowing red eyes, black hair, and razor-like teeth, and it was looking down at me with immense hatred.

I jumped right out of bed, frightened so badly I was shaking. What had I seen and why? Things in my life were turning really ugly. Was this God's way of answering my prayers? All these years of adhering to New Age philosophy, with all its supposed glimmer and warmth, was looking a lot different. I no longer felt safe. However, I was desperately seeking peace and still went to my favorite yoga class. My next session would be different, though.

As I rushed to my class, arriving late as usual, I sneaked in while everyone had already begun warming up. As I was putting away my shoes, the atmosphere felt different to me. I mean, the room was dark, candles lit, and the strong aroma of incense filled the air—all normal occurrences—but I was sensing spiritual energy this evening. The air felt thick, and I felt uncomfortable there for the first time.

The instructor that night seemed to brim with a spiritual spark and was showering her students with adoration while praising kundalini and shakti energy. As I moved throughout the yoga sequence, I couldn't help but notice the many Hindu statues sitting prominently in the corners of the room. For the first time, I had an inner knowing that these idols were only representing demons. In that moment, I saw the lady next to me moving into poses, and she almost seemed to be in a trance while letting out strange moans.

My teacher appeared to be filled with such bliss and gave loving, kind words to everyone, but I saw something deeper, more sinister that night. I could sense in that moment that the source of all this energy and peace had much darker origins. I was feeling more awake. I was seeing through a broad deception, and I did not feel right about returning to this yoga class. I couldn't believe what I was seeing. Was God answering my prayers? I was always truth seeking, and my seeking was coming full circle, but the answers terrified me.

One day, while searching online, I found a website speaking of chakras, and to my surprise it was a satanic website! This concerned me. Opening your chakras seemed to open you up to the spiritual realm. These were your psychic centers, and it worked well with Satanism/Luciferiansm. I was starting to think our chakras were meant to be closed. If I was a Christian, would I want to be partaking in the same spirituality as Satanists? My world seemed to further come crashing down. I continued trying to read the Bible but was still being tormented at night with visions. Everything I was learning was shaking me up, and I had never felt so confused.

One day I was home by myself and felt drowsy, so I decided to lay down on the couch and take a nap. I was right in between sleeping and being awake when I felt some entity come over and touch me right on the forehead, where your third eye would be. Again, frightened, I woke up and knew I was no longer alone.

The periods of random disorientation continued, and I started to have a weird sensation in my spine. It would feel like a cold liquid climbing up the base of my spine. Other times, I suffered with intense back pain but would chalk it up to having previous back labors with my children—that is until the vibrations in my lower back started.

As I began getting ready in my bathroom one afternoon, I had this feeling of dread come over me and sensed a presence around me. My back had been hurting for weeks, and I started to feel this sensation further climb my back. Out of fear, I began to scream for Jesus to make it all stop! I had had enough; I didn't want to feel like this anymore.

In a matter of seconds, the sensations in my back stopped. As I began to move around, my back was no longer in pain. My prayer to Jesus had stopped this kundalini energy immediately! I fell to the floor, crying. It was all crystal clear to me now. None of this New Age stuff was from God. Everything I was doing was opposed to God. I remembered my initial prayer to God when I had started this yoga journey. I had asked Him if this is what I should do, and is it compatible with Christianity? The Lord was revealing to me an unequivocal, NO!

As the days went on, it was as if blinders were being taken off my eyes. Thank God I could now see. Everything occult and New Age was a lie: a beautiful deception. Such an intricate web was being woven over those who did not love the truth. I was thankful that day that all the sensations in my back stopped, but I was horrified about what I was finding out. So many questions circled my mind. What do I do now? What would my future be? And how would I help those struggling with mental illness and addictions? Would I give them medication?

My discovery that New Age was a false truth was heartbreaking. It's as if a veil was being lifted from my eyes, and I didn't like what I was seeing. My entire world came crashing down. Even though it was God leading me into truth, I couldn't help feeling angry at Him. How could He allow such lies? Even though it hurt, I refused to give in to temptation, and I knew I needed to know God and know Him on His own terms, not some false spirituality I thought I could weave Him into.

Again, my spirit plunged to the depths of depression. All I could do was cry out to God and open the Bible, desperately trying to understand. Sometimes reading Psalms and praying brought a slight peace over me, and I could get through the day with my anxiety.

This was a very painful time in my life, a time where I would be forced to confront truth, even when it was the last thing I ever wanted to hear. Jesus was exclusive, and He was not compatible with any other belief system. New agers often spoke of a Christ consciousness, but this was nothing more than becoming a god yourself. I was seeing the New Age and occult as nothing more than the first lie ever told in the Garden of Eden.

(Genesis 3:4) Ye shall be as god's, ye shall not die.

* * *

The next couple of months of my life, I was focused intensely on research. I could hardly believe all that was being revealed to me. Everything was becoming crystal clear. Jesus was calling me out of darkness, to be His own, and what a narrow path it would be. I knew there was no turning back. I was going to follow Jesus, wherever that would lead me.

CHAPTER 6
PEELING BACK THE LAYERS

(Genesis 3:5)
For God does know that in the day you eat
from it your eyes shall be opened, and you will be
like God, knowing good and evil.

Reality came crashing in. Everything I thought I believed up until this point was a lie. I was happy to have found the truth that is in Jesus, but that still didn't make it any easier. I wanted truth, but with truth comes much sorrow. Intuitively I knew God was answering my prayers, but the answer wasn't what I had been expecting. Truth was not subjective like the New Age would have you believe. Truth was exclusive; truth was a person—His name was JESUS! His Holy Spirit was known as the Spirt of Truth, and He was beginning to work in my life and lead me down a path of awakening that I could never have imagined. It was time to peel back the layers of an intricately woven web of lies. Over the next few months, I began digging into research to find answers to what I had experienced.

The darkness, fear and oppression/depression that had clouded my life came by way of my involvement in the occult. Yoga opened me up to a kundalini awakening. The energy surges through my body and spine, the visions, sleep paralysis, and paranormal happenings, were all symptoms of kundalini awakening. This is the primary goal of yoga; this leads to enlightenment.

So, what is yoga? I mean, here in the West it is touted as an everyday fix and exercise for just about everything. Once it made its way over here, it exploded in epic proportions. How could something gain popularity so fast? It has changed our collective consciousness and is leading to a real paradigm shift. Yoga and meditation are taught in schools; prisons; hospitals; and even our military, often used for PTSD. No one even mentions the dangers that can arise from this change in consciousness.

Yoga is a form of Hinduism, but it is packaged in such a way that it seems neutral—no matter what religion you practice, it's okay. It has been the catalyst to change our thoughts and even unite our beliefs.

The word "yoga" means "to yoke or union." The very definition of yoga, according to Merriam Webster's dictionary, is this: *"A Hindu theistic philosophy teaching suppression of all activity of the mind, body, and will in order that the self may realize it's distinction from them and attain liberation."*

I'm not sure if that's what people are signing up for when they are joining a yoga class. If we are giving up all activity of our mind, will, and body, then who or what is taking control? The goal of Eastern meditation is to empty one's mind. That's very different from the goal of Biblical meditation, which would never require us to empty our minds but to fill it with meditation on God's word.

Yoga is an entire system combining breath, meditation, and postures to bring about a very specific goal: enlightenment, or samadhi. Enlightenment is a process that allows you to realize the divinity within and escape the endless cycles of reincarnation. Enlightenment is a conscious annihilation, it's a way of dying to yourself, and being reborn.

"According to yoga philosophy, it is through ignorance that the soul has been joined with nature. The aim is to get rid of nature's control over us. That is the goal of all religions. Each soul is potentially divine. The goal is to manifest the divinity within, by controlling nature, external and internal. The yogi tries to reach this goal through

psychic control." (The Yoga Sutras of Patanjali, Vivekananda, Chapter 2, Section 818.)

Trying to manifest the divine within while controlling internal and external forces sounds much like the first lie ever told, *"Ye shall be as gods," (Genesis 3:4)*.

This entire philosophy is directly opposed to what Christianity teaches. We are sinners; there is nothing within us that is not wicked. In the Christian worldview, we needed a way back to God, so God sent His only begotten son to die on a cross and defeat sin. In Christianity, we accept Jesus and surrender our lives to Him. This enables us to receive HIS Holy Spirit, who comes and seals up our spirit with His until we die and leave this earth.

(Hebrews 9:27) And as it is appointed for men to die once, but after this the judgment...

There is no room for reincarnation in the Christian worldview. There is no need for enlightenment or striving to reach a state of nirvana. Yet, so many professing Christians are practicing yoga, and even many churches now offer "Christian" yoga classes. Yoga is a way to open yourself up spiritually, by opening our chakras, or energy centers. Sometimes chakras are wheels of energy. Does the Bible ever mention this? We will look at that later.

According to The Yoga Sutras of Patanjali, there is power that can be gained from this spiritual practice. In fact, with the system of yoga, one can obtain powers.

"When one has succeeded in making samyama, all powers come under His control. This is the great instrument of the yogi." (The Yoga Sutras of Patanjali, Vivekananda, Chapter 3, Section 1020.)

The yogi attains samyama, which is infinite energy at his disposal. By the process of mortification to the body, the yogi can have *"heightened powers of vision, hearing things at a distance and so on." (The Yoga Sutras of Patanjali, Vivekananda, Chapter 2, Section 941.)*

According to *"The Yoga Sutras of Patanjali,"* This is said about repetition of mantras: *"By repetition of a mantra comes the realization of intended deity. The higher the beings you want to get, the more you practice." (Vivekananda, chapter 2, Section 941.)*

Here in the West, more and more people are being taught to repeat a mantra, maybe even chant; all with very little knowing of what any of this means. *"The Yoga Sutras of Patanjali,"* paint a very different picture of what yoga entails. But it is far from an exercise. It is a spiritual, religious practice, one that should come with warnings.

Yoga is really nothing more than an occult art, used to open yourself up to the spirit realm. As we will see, asanas and pranayama, combined with meditation, are used as a recipe to open channels and nerve currents within your body. Asanas are a comfortable seated position, used to decrease restlessness during meditation.

Next is the prana, which is achieved after the asana is conquered. *"Prana is thought of as the sum total of cosmic energy that is in each body, and the most apparent manifestation is the motion of the lungs." (The Yoga Sutras of Patanjali, Vivekananda, Chapter 2, Section 961.)*

Pranayama is the motion of our breath, which gains control of the prana. The point of pranayama is controlling the nadi currents through the aid of controlled pulsation of the right and left lung. According to *"The Yoga Sutras of Patanjali,"* when someone has succeeded in making this samyama, *"all powers are under his control."* Samayama is concentration, and when that is combined with Dhyana (meditation), plus samadhi (union), this enables a process of psychological absorption in the object of meditation. One can use the power of their concentrated mind to obtain whatever they desire.

The Yoga Sutras mention a light that can be seen emanating from the top of the head. Siddhas can be thought of as enlightened beings. *"The siddhas are beings who are a little above ghost." (The Yoga Sutras of Patanjali, Vivekananda, Chapter 3, Section 1135.)*

In occult teachings, siddhas are, *"Spirits in the sense of an individual or conscious spirit—of great sages from spheres of higher planes, who voluntarily incarnate in mortal bodies to help the human race in their upward progress." (The Secret Doctrine: Anthropogenesis, Helena Blavatsky, Page 673.)*

This is very interesting to read, considering that in the West we have been brainwashed to think of yoga as only exercise, when what I just described is *possession*.

Siddhas are also seen as supernatural powers attained by yogis as they master the eight-fold path. The eight-fold path is a Buddhist practice that leads to liberation from samsara, which is the painful path of reincarnation. As I have already described, this is a very religious teaching, and it contradicts Christianity completely.

Siddha not only describes powers attained, but it also can be used as a term in Indian culture to mean "wise man," and "perfected one." These Siddha masters are men who have attained a high degree of spiritual and physical perfection. Siddha teachers use a method called "shaktipat" to initiate. Using this method, a guru can transfer his immense spiritual energy to his disciples by a mere glance or touch and completely transform them. This spiritual-energy transfer is known as "the serpent energy" or awakening of the kundalini.

"Spiritual awakening lies at the heart of the mystical journey. This infusion of energy from the spiritual master to the seeker brings about the awakening of the seeker's own inerrant power, called "kundalini." Shaktipat is described by the yogic texts as an "initiation that activates an inner unfolding of awareness that leads to progressively higher states of consciousness." (Siddhayogapath.com, Shaktipat Initiation.)

This awakening, I unknowingly brought upon myself by dabbling in the occult and yoga practice. What's frightening is that *churches* have embraced yoga, and there has been an influx of New Age spirituality. Later on, we will discuss what is known as the "holy spirit." It might be kundalini energy being transferred by shaktipat methods.

Let's repeat what kundalini is: Kundalini is very important in Hinduism. It is thought of as a serpent energy that lies dormant at the base of one's spine. As it awakens, it springs upward through your spine, reaching all the chakras until it reaches your crown chakra.

"Chakras in Hinduism are considered part of the esoteric anatomy. They are interconnected with nadis, which are meridian-type channels that carry energy around the body. Chakras interface with other energy bodies to assist in raising the kundalini, an energy that invites union with the divine," (Dale 2009, Page 237.)

Many people in the West even believe that kundalini is some biological energy that we harness. However, in Hinduism, this energy is *"part of a process of evolving into a union with a deity." (The Subtle Body: An Encyclopedia of your Energetic Anatomy, Cyndi Dale, Page 237.)*

A deity is a god. Yoga connects your own soul and body with an unknown, mystical force or god. Now, for a Christian, to connect yourself with anything other than the God of the Bible is connecting yourself to demonic powers.

The West has adopted many Eastern practices, and we accept everything as neutral, or even natural, but seem ignorant to the fact that what is being spread has its roots in the occult and Satanism.

"Shakti lies within us all, coiled within our root chakra in the guise of a serpent. kundalini shakti is the power at rest. Her goal is to rejoin her great love, Shiva, who resides in the seventh chakra. When unified, the two create supreme consciousness. kundalini frees the graduate from the confines of the physical body. Powers arise, mystical abilities awaken. And the soul is freed from the wheel of life that forces reincarnation." (The Subtle Body: An Encyclopedia of your Energetic Anatomy, Cyndi Dale, Page 241.)

Kundalini works by activation of certain energies in the human body. It opens the chakras, or energy centers; the nadis, which are streams or conduits; the koshas, which are veils of energy that contain the spirit and then works through subtle bodies, which are the energy bodies that contain the human and spiritual dimensions. This form of energy is seen throughout many spiritual traditions throughout the world. But what we are seeing now is chakras moving to another discipline, and that is science.

With activation of these powers, it leads to mystical abilities: the power to become invisible, levitate, healing capabilities, and even enter another body or mind. Kundalini travels through the spine like a double helix shape, the same as how DNA works. It changes the spiritual makeup of a person.

God has sealed the human body in such a way that it is not meant to be tampered with. Engaging in these occult methods are opening up souls and detaching the mind from the body. It is producing a similar process as death. It is believed that near death experiences happen because, near death, it is kundalini energy that rushes through the body.

Here is one account from the International Association for Near Death Studies:

"In 1974 I activated kundalini through meditation, but I did not know what I was doing. It erupted big time and blew my mind away. It was scary. I had a health problem in my ears, and I was in a very bad car accident, so I meditated several hours a day.

I first noticed kundalini rising in my head. It slowly moved down to my tail bone. After that all hell broke loose, my heart stopped beating, and I stopped breathing. I said, "Oh Jesus," and all of a sudden, I popped out of my body.

The next thing I knew, I was hovering over a shore about 100 to 300 feet in the air. I could see the water, it was deep blue, and the sand was white. I didn't see any people. Across the water, I saw a mountain range with trees and grass. I thought, this looks nice. Then I noticed I couldn't see my body. I got a mental impression, like someone was telling me that my body was back on planet earth!

I said, 'Where am I?'

The voice said, 'You're on another planet!'

'What about my body?' I asked.

The answer I got was, 'If they find it, they'll bury it like any other dead body!'

Then I said, 'This is what's known as death.' I thought that this was a strange turn of events.

I looked across the lake and saw a white sailboat. I wanted to go to it and see if any people were on it.

Then the voice said, 'You can't stay; you're not done yet.'
I thought, Done with what?
The next thing I knew, I was back in my body, gasping for
air, and my heart started pounding."

This is a very dangerous practice, and not one that should be taken lightly. If we go back to the very first book of the Bible, Genesis, we see the serpent's very first lie given to Adam and Eve. In every culture and religion, the "serpent" and "dragon worship" are something they all have in common. Only one religion, the Hebrew-Christian view, sees the serpent as the devil, the old dragon that deceives the whole world.

(Genesis 3:1-6) Now the serpent was more cunning than any other beast of the field which the Lord God had made. And he said to the woman, "Has God indeed said, 'You shall not eat of every tree of the garden?'"

Eve then responded that if she would eat of this forbidden fruit that they would die.

But the deceitful serpent said to the woman, "You will not surely die. For God knows that the day you eat of it your eyes will be opened, and you will be like God, knowing good and evil."

So, when the woman saw that the tree was good for food, that it was pleasant to the eyes, and a tree desirable to make one wise, she took of its fruit and ate.

This is the oldest and one of the most effective lies. It speaks to man's desire to be a god, apart from the one true God.

As I mentioned earlier, sometimes chakras are described as wheels of light. They are subtle energy bodies along the spine. Not only do they emit energy, they receive energy.

"Chakras are considered physical as well as subtle and are considered the foundation of all existence, psychologically and physically." (The Subtle Body: An Encyclopedia of your Energetic Anatomy, Cyndi Dale, Page 251.)

Now, we know that the human body is composed of energy. We have a nervous system, a heart that works from electrical currents, and an energy system that causes blood to flow. There is believed to be nadis, which are channels of energy. Shushma nadi is considered a central nadi that is responsible for energy that passes along the spinal cord.

"*There are three main nadis, shushma (main nadi), Ida (left side of body), and pingala (right side of body.) For their part, the Ida and Pingala nadi cross like a double helix and relate to the sympathetic nervous trunks on both sides of the spinal cord. Together, these three nadis interact to cleanse the physical body and stimulate the rising of the kundalini through the spinal cord. If done appropriately, this process also unfolds the siddhi, or seemingly magical gifts.*" (*The Subtle Body: An Encyclopedia of your Energetic Anatomy, Cyndi Dale Page 274.*)

We can visualize the shape of this energy from the kundalini caduceus, which is often used as a symbol in medical practice. Kundalini is a process that involves the most important aspect of the human body, the spinal cord, and the nervous system: breath, organs, mind and consciousness. This manipulation of energy to both mind, body, and spirit is a process: an almost forbidden practice that is opening up our spirits in a way that is not meant to be opened. The Bible does not mention "chakras" nor "kundalini," but it mentions a serpent, one who promises the knowledge of good and evil.

Now, here is what the Bible mentions: (*Ecclesiastes 12:6*) *Remember your creator earnestly now, before the silver cord be loosed, or the golden bowl be broken, or the pitcher be broken at the fountain, or the wheel broken at the cistern.*

This verse is understood to be the process of death. The silver cord is the spinal cord: the golden bowl, the membranes of the brain; the pitcher refers to the spring of life, or the arteries, and the wheel broken at the cistern represents the ceasing of the pulse and conveying blood to the left ventricle.

It is interesting to note that kundalini is tampering with these same processes that create death. The kundalini process is working to loosen one's soul, consciousness, and mind as separate from the body. Therefore, some NDE's (near death experiences) seem almost like a kundalini awakening. Often yogi's and serious practitioners can learn to stop their breath, pulse, and heartbeat with meditation, at will.

Learning to control your natural life forces at will and enter into spiritual realms, with seemingly magical abilities, is exactly what the serpent in the Garden of Eden promised: *(Genesis 3:5) You shall become as gods.*

Entering this occult world is the antithesis to everything the God of the Bible commands and everything He despises. The path of yoga is so much more than what meets the eye. It starts out as an exercise that then dangles a carrot in front of you to then seek more. It makes us feel good, so it must be good. This is farthest from the truth. The apple in the Garden of Eden looked good too, but, in the end, it caused death, physical and spiritual. To follow Jesus is to follow the narrow path.

(Matthew 7:13) Enter by the narrow gate; for wide is the gate and broad is the way that leads to destruction, and there are many who go in by it.

We have an enemy that is prowling, waiting to devour us, one that will stop at nothing to get us off the only path to life. He shows us many seemingly good paths that concentrate on our own selves by going within. Even Christians are falling for this ancient practice, trying to somehow invent their own spirituality for getting closer to God.

We need to stop and ask, "Would God approve of this? Would this look pleasing in His sight?" I warn against putting a Christian nametag on anything that has its roots in another religion. *(Exodus 34:14) Our God is a jealous God, and you are to have no gods before Him.* Each yoga pose is offering you up to a Hindu deity. You are opening your body and soul up to evil entities.

(2 Corinthians 11:14) And no wonder, for Satan himself masquerades as an angel of light.

Even the history of yoga coming to the West is filled with deception and void of honesty. Yoga is a 3000-year-old practice that originated in the East, by very religious teachers, as a way to induce death. It became popularized in the West in the 60's, alongside the psychedelic drug culture, and was introduced as a way of life. This began a transcendental experience, one that could alter our consciousness the same way as hallucinogenic drugs could. The history of yoga is very lengthy and vast. We will touch base on a few of its gurus that brought it to the United states.

In 1893, Swami Vivekananda made his way to the Parliament of World Religions at the Art Institute of Chicago. He would give his first lecture on September 11th.

"Though initially nervous, he bowed to Saraswati, the Hindu goddess of learning, and he felt he got new energy in his body; he felt someone or something else occupied his body—the soul of India, the echo of the rishis, the voice of Ramakrishna, the mouthpiece of the resurgent time spirit." (Swami Vivekananda's Birthday, Shepparton InterfaithNetwork.org, 2016.)

Vivekananda received a standing ovation. His address was one of unity and that all religions lead to the same path. He went on to quote, *"As different streams having their sources in different paths which men take through different tendencies, various as they appear, crooked or straight, all lead to thee." (Swami Vivekananda on Truth in all Religions in Welcoming Participants to the World Parliament of Religions, Berkleycenter.georgetown.edu)*

This speech would start the infiltration of Hinduism and Buddhism into the West. The New Age movement was beginning to be established.

Christianity has been banned from many public arenas, but other religions are widely accepted in parliament. In India, by law, no Christian missionary activity is allowed there; meanwhile, Hindu missionaries are busy here, launching the greatest missionary effort known.

In January 1979, at the VHP-sponsored second "World Congress on Hinduism" in Allahabad, India, attended by about 60,000 delegates from around the world, a speaker declared, *"Our mission in the West has been crowned with fantastic success. Hinduism is becoming the dominant world religion, and the end of Christianity has come near," (Yoga and the Body of Christ, Dave Hunt, Page 9.)*

The Vishwa Hindu Parashad of America has its own missionary activities and even works to reconvert people back to Hinduism.

"The VHP of America conducted the World Vision 2000 conference in Washington D.C. in 1993, which became a rallying point for overseas Hindus and a ground for further recruitment. The VHP's success can be primarily in terms of financial clout—as the primary mode of channelling dollars into Hindutva politics back in India. The council that was started in Bombay, Maharastra with a political objective of establishing the supremacy of Hinduism all over the globe. In India, it has organized several massacres against Christians and Muslims. It is in the forefront in the call for a Hindu Rashtra, a Hindu state, ethnically cleansed of its non-Aryan populations." (VHP: World Hindu Council, SikhiWiki.org)

Here in the US, not only are we pushing Christianity away from all facets of life, we are accepting other religions in the deceptive name of health, science, and exercise, ignoring its bitter root while also funding US dollars to these countries.

Now, don't get me wrong, America is a place of religious freedom. However, when other religions are coming in, and are even welcomed in government and politics with open arms, while Biblical Christianity is pushed away as intolerant, then it is time to revaluate what the agenda truly is here. Christians in the West are embracing beliefs other than our Christian roots and thinking they can somehow incorporate everything as one. The entire face of Christianity is changing because God's children are lacking wisdom and failing to take God's word seriously.

(Hosea 4:6) My people are destroyed for lack of knowledge. Because you have rejected knowledge, I will also reject you from being my priest for me.

So many are professing Christians, but so few are walking with Christ. Walking with Christ is a narrow path. Any wisdom gained from a source other than our Savior is from the world.

(1 Corinthians 3:19) For wisdom of this world is foolishness in God's sight. As it is written: "He catches the wise in their craftiness.

As Christians, we must consider the source of any "truth." Things like yoga and the New Age are cleverly packaged and appear to hold a universal wisdom to their teachings, but we must ask ourselves where these teachings originate from. So many gurus have come spreading their "truth," but let me assure you, their motives are far more sinister than they look.

Take, for example, transcendental meditation. TM is a movement founded by Maharishi Mahesh Yogi, who spread his deep meditation practice around the world. In the 1970s, the TM movement became part of hippie sub-culture. Maharishi would declare the year 1959—the year he began teaching his method— "The Year of Global Awakening."

One of the most famous advocates for TM were The Beatles, who happened to spend several weeks studying with Maharishi at a retreat in India.

"Maharishi Mahesh Yogi kept working tirelessly touring the world, writing books, certifying over 40,000 meditation teachers, setting up TM centers, schools and universities." (tmhome.com, 2015.)

He was also one of the first gurus to encourage modern scientific research to study the effects of his brand of meditation. Was Maharishi's goal only health and wellness though? In 1981, at a transcendental meditation conference in India, a TM spokesman stated: *"The entire mission of TM is to counter the ever-spreading demon of Christianity."* Based on this statement, The Eastern practitioners had a goal of religious persuasion, not health and fitness.

Let us not forget that one of the key goals of meditation is an altered state of consciousness. They advertise TM as an answer to stress relief, better work performance, healthy blood pressure, lowered risk of heart disease, and treatment for alcohol/drug abuse. But what isn't mentioned is its religious undertones and the opening of your mind and soul to spiritual experiences. It is not some exercise; it has a spiritual component that cannot be forgotten. It is a meditation that involves completely shutting off your mind while consistently repeating a mantra.

We know from reading the Yoga Sutras, that mantras equal calling on a deity. You are calling on some entity while leaving your mind blank. What research and science forget to tell us is the many demonic experiences that some people have had from practicing TM yoga.

An altered state of consciousness... its what society seems to strive for. It's interesting to note that the term 'altered state of consciousness' used to be known as the term, "possession states." Your mind has then shifted; it has been altered in some way that is no longer natural.

In TM meditation, its founder and other gurus like him live different lives than what they preach, often involved in scandals, greed, spiritual pride, lust, and dishonesty. Many of these gurus teach a life of asceticism, getting rid of your ego, and even pretend to be holy by remaining celibate. Bikram Choudbury, founder of Bikram yoga, had five women file suits against him, ranging from sexual assault to rape.

John Friend, founder of Anusara Yoga was found guilty of leading a Wiccan coven, while also having affairs with married students and teachers.

Amit Desai, founder of Kripalu Center, confessed to three affairs and was forced to resign from his own ashram.

Bhagwan Shree Rajnees was involved in a little of everything: prostitution, drug-running, drug use, and worked his followers to the bone. In India, he was known as the "sex guru." Here in the States, he was known as the "Rolls-Royce guru," owning more than 90 at a time.

Maharishi Mahesh yogi, the leader of TM, has been accused of seducing several of his followers. The Beatles broke ties with him over accusations of trying to rape Mia Farrow. Marharishi had amassed a fortune in the West and lived in a luxurious two hundred room mansion. (*A List of Yoga Scandals Involving Gurus, Teachers, Students, Sex, and Other Inappropriate Behavior," Kara Leah Grant, Https://theyogalunchbox.co.nz/tag/jivamutki 2015.*)

These are a few of the many scandals involving yoga gurus. These are deceitful men that have come to the West to brainwash a wealthy society while being worshipped by their victims as godmen. It's very sad to watch millions of people line up to be deceived, worshipping men as god's, and trying to attain some pseudo-spiritual state that can only lead to psychological harm.

TM is a dangerous practice, and it is no secret that harmful effects have been talked about in medical and psychological circles. In "*The Buddha Pill*," a book written by psychologists, Dr. Miguel Farias and Catharine Wikholm, show that 60% of people who have been on a meditation retreat have suffered at least one negative side effect, while one in fourteen have suffered "profoundly adverse effects."

A former TM teacher, Joe Kellett, states that, "*TM can increase anxiety in some people, which is well known as, 'relaxation induced anxiety.'*"

There are many examples of how TMers experience "induced psychosis." TM can cause a host of symptoms, ranging from physical to emotional problems. For physical effects, it can cause uncontrollable fatigue, insomnia, stomach problems, chronic neck and back pain, chronic headaches, menstrual issues, and involuntary body movements.

For emotional problems, it can cause anxiety; fear; obsessive ideas, disassociation and pseudo identity (similar to multiple personality disorder); suicidal ideation, gestures or successful attempts; nervous breakdown; psychosis; depression; avoidance; delusional thinking; and auditory and visual hallucinations.

It amazes me that these adverse effects can be the result of trying to find simple relaxation. Being in the New Age for so many years, I had suffered consequences from meditation and kundalini energy. Working in the mental health field, I saw so many of these modalities being used to bring health, peace, and happiness. But what about the side effects? These are never mentioned, and unsuspecting people are never warned. There is plenty of research in transpersonal psychology that documents harmful effects of TM and kundalini phenomenon.

In the International Journal of Psychotherapy, in an article titled, "*Meditation: concepts, effects and uses in therapy,*" a German study is done, and many side effects are listed.

"Not all effects of the practice of meditation are beneficial. Shapiro (1992) found that 62.9% of the subjects reported adverse effects during and after meditation, and 7.4% experienced profoundly adverse effects. The length of practice did not make any difference to the quality and frequency of adverse effects. These adverse effects were relaxation-induced anxiety and panic; paradoxical increases in tension; less motivation in life; boredom; pain; impaired reality testing; confusion and disorientation; feeling 'spaced out'; depression; increased negativity; being more judgemental; and, ironically, feeling addicted to meditation."

(Craven, 1989) "Other adverse effects described are uncomfortable kinaesthetic sensations, mild disassociation, feelings of guilt and, via anxiety-provoking phenomena, psychosis-like symptoms, grandiosity, elation, destructive behavior and suicidal feelings." This is one study of many that are available.

Another lesser-known issue is the legal ramifications regarding the cult that is TM. An affidavit from a former MIU legal counsel and former director of grants administration, had these excerpts to say:

"A disturbing denial or avoidance syndrome, and even outright lies and deception, are used to cover up or sanitize the dangerous reality on campus of very serious nervous breakdowns, episodes of dangerous and bizarre behavior, suicidal and homicidal ideation, threats and attempts, psychotic episodes, crime, depression, and manic behavior that often accompanied roundings (intensive group meditations with brainwashing techniques.)"

"The consequences of intensive, or even regular, meditation was so damaging and disruptive to the nervous system that students could not enrol in or continue with regular academic programs."

"He (Maharishi) was aware, apparently for some time, of the problem: suicide attempts, assaults, homicidal ideation, serious psychotic episodes, depressions, inter alia, but his general attitude was to leave it alone or conceal it because the community would lose faith in the TM movement." (The Healing Gods: Complementary and Alternative Medicine in Christian America, Candy Brown, Page 134.)

Besides the research that documents all the adverse effects, there are also plenty of lawsuits against the TM organization. In one civil suit, in 1986, Robert Kropinski files a suit for psychological damage and wins.

Kropinski, Robert. United States District Court for the District of Columbia. Civil Suit #85-2848, 1986: *"In his civil suit against the TM Organization, Kropinski reported incidents of alleged psychosis, suicides, and the drugging of course participants. The court document "Answers to Defendants' Interrogatories—John Doe I" contained this list of TM victims. A Washington, D.C. jury awarded Robert Kropinski, 39, $137,890 to pay for his psychiatric treatment.* Kropinski was an 11-year member who was part of Maharishi's personal entourage." *(Dangers of Meditation, svarasa.com.)*

Looking at some research and lawsuits, a very different picture begins to appear regarding the peaceful claims of meditation. Studies would have the public believe that practices such as this are always an answer to stress relief and better brain power. Just like any drug prescribed, isn't it dishonest to not mention adverse effects? People often forget that these are spiritual practices, ones that open our mind and spirit up to a very real spiritual realm.

As a Christian, Biblical meditation is always turning our thoughts towards God's word, not emptying our mind and putting us in an altered state of consciousness.

(Joshua 1:8) This book of the Law shall not depart from your mouth, but you shall meditate on it day and night so that you may be careful to do according to all that is written in it. For then you will make your way prosperous, and then you will have good success.

(Psalm 19:14) Let the words of my mouth and the meditation of my heart be acceptable in your sight, O Lord, my rock and my redeemer.

When I give my thoughts and will over to Jesus and renew my mind with His word, I never have to worry about any psychological harm. I am safe within His arms. I never have to worry about my prayer practice becoming dangerous, unlike when I had a kundalini awakening.

Kundalini is a very well-known phenomenon to those who work in the field of transpersonal psychology. The famous psychoanalyst, Carl Jung, was a pioneer in bringing the Eastern world into psychology. Carl Jung wrote popular books such as, "*Psychology of Kundalini Yoga*"; "*Four Archetypes*"; and "*Psychology and the Occult*," to name a few. Carl Jung was a Swiss psychologist who brought the Eastern concept of higher consciousness to the Western world. Jung claimed that the symbolism of kundalini yoga suggested that the bizarre symptomology that patients at times presented resulted from the awakening of the kundalini.

Jung even visited India, and in his book "*The Psychology of Kundalini*," a friend who accompanies Jung recalls some of the imagery he encountered: "*As we go through temples of Kali, which were numerous at almost every Hindu city, we saw evidence of animal sacrifice; the places were filthy, dirty-dried blood on the floor and lots of remains of red betlenut all around, so that the colour of red was associated with destructiveness. Concurrently, in Calcutta, Jung began to have a series of dreams in which the colour red was stressed. It wasn't long before dysentery overcame Jung, and I had to take him to the hospital in Calcutta… A more lasting effect of this impression of the destructiveness of Kali was the emotional foundation it gave him for the conviction that evil was not a negative thing but a positive thing…*"

Carl Jung devoted much time immersing himself in Eastern culture and the study of kundalini phenomenon, enough so that he understood the exceptional dangers associated with the awakening of the serpent power. He often cautioned European practitioners, as they could often become hypnotized by it.

"*For Jung, the danger was one of mimetic madness: the European who practices yoga does not know what he is doing. It has a bad effect on him; sooner or later he becomes afraid and sometimes it even leads him over the edge of madness.*" (*The Psychology of Kundalini Yoga, C.G. Jung, Pg. 30*)

Jung also concludes and predicts that the West will develop their own form of yoga, one that will be laid down by Christianity. That prediction has in fact come true. Many Christians practice

Yoga, and many churches even offer their own "Holy Yoga," without ever considering its occult root. If we continue to mix the occult with Christianity, what type of fruit will be produced? Yoga is cloaked in peace and innocence, but the spiritual dangers are hidden from plain view. In fact, later in life, Jung himself experienced madness from exploring the Eastern world and became psychotic, often visited by dead people and hearing voices.

Carl Jung considers the *"Tibetan Book of the Dead"* to be a "process of initiation." Jung writes: *"One often hears and reads about the dangers of yoga, particularly of the ill-reputed kundalini yoga. The deliberately induced psychotic state, which in certain unstable individuals might easily lead to a real psychosis, is a danger that needs to be taken seriously indeed. These things really are dangerous and ought not to be meddled with in our typically Western way. It is meddling with fate, which strikes at the very roots of human existence and can let loose a flood of sufferings of which no sane person ever dreamed." (Jung on Death and Immortality, C.G. Jung, Pg., 31)*

Carl Jung was a pioneer in psychology for introducing Eastern methods, but even he was aware of the dangers involved. Westerners today would never even dream of such dangers while engaging in meditation and yoga.

As I was becoming aware of my own kundalini awakening, and on the edge of madness, I started to seek answers. As someone who planned at the time to go into psychiatry, I was shocked to know that the phenomenon of kundalini was mentioned in the "DSM IV" (The Diagnostic and Statistical Manual.) This is the book in psychiatry that has all the psychiatric diagnoses. What I stumbled upon was something called, "kundalini syndrome." This was a syndrome that people would experience, characterized by psychotic-like symptoms, and end up in the psych ward.

Fast forward a few years later and that name has changed, and now it is categorized as a spiritual crisis. It is known as physio-kundalini syndrome, identified by psychotic-like features displayed in sufferers. Transpersonal psychologists have characterized this phenomenon as a "spiritual emergency."

The DSM IV made this diagnostic step to differentiate between a spiritual issue or psychotic disorder. There has been a long-shared history between mysticism and psychotic disorders. If something is deemed as spiritual, such as kundalini, it is seen in the psychology field as having growth potential: seen as a force that can destroy in order to re-create.

In 1977, a bio medical engineer, named Itzhak Bentov, studied the physiological effects of altered states of consciousness. Bentov concluded that, *"The normal biological evolution of the human nervous system could be accelerated under certain circumstances, triggering a predictable sequence of physiological stresses on the body that he described as a progressive sensory-motor cortex syndrome. While Bentov acknowledged that the concept of kundalini involves spiritual forces and effects beyond these physiological symptoms, he proposed a limited mechanical-physiological portion of kundalini syndrome as a working model." (The Physio-Kundalini Syndrome and Mental Illness, Bruce Greyson, The Journal of Transpersonal Psychology," Page 44.)*

The physio-kundalini model was recognized because therapists wanted to be able to recognize clients going through a spiritual awakening rather than be labelled mentally ill. In physio-kundalini syndrome, some of the phenomenon resembles that of schizophrenia.

"For example, hearing voices, becoming locked into unusual postures, sudden intense mood swings for no apparent reason, and thoughts speeding up or slowing down. However, there are typical physio-kundalini phenomena that don't share schizophrenia-like traits. These are symptoms such as pockets of extreme body temperature, changes in breathing, specific localized pain, expanding beyond body, out-of-body experiences, deep ecstatic tickles, internal lights or colors, and an ascending anatomic progression of symptoms." (The Physio-kundalini Syndrome and Mental Illness, Bruce Grayson, The Journal of Transpersonal Psychology 1993, Page 48.)

According to psychologist, David Lukoff, he recommended that, *"Psychotic symptoms in the context of kundalini experiences be diagnosed not as schizophrenia, but as 'mystical experience with psychotic features,' with the implication that this condition can have a positive outcome." (Physio-kundalini Syndrome and Mental Illness, Bruce Greyson, The Journal of Transpersonal Psychology, 1993, Page 56.)*

As someone who started to develop kundalini awakening, I can assure you the experience became frightening and destabilizing. The realization that this was a phenomenon, spoken of even in psychology, alerted me and validated what I was experiencing.

The very fact that some people could end up in psychiatric wards because of "enlightenment" was terrifying to me. Calling upon the name of Jesus made my symptoms start to disappear. The presence of Jesus was a calming presence, not one of spiritual destruction. The God I was coming to know was someone I could trust, someone who comforted and, most of all, wasn't some God who I could awaken within to cause some pseudo-spiritual, born-again experience.

(2 Timothy 1:7) For God has not given us the spirit of fear, but of power, and of love, and of a sound mind.

Any force that causes a spirit of fear and ruins one's psyche is not from God but, in fact, is more like the antichrist spirit, the same spirit of the serpent who promised the forbidden fruit in the Garden of Eden: a rotten fruit, one that separates you from the very breath of God while promising you can be your own god, ending the reincarnation cycle.

For the serpent said in the Garden to Eden, *"You will not surely die." (Genesis 3:4.)*

When awakening kundalini, we are invoking our power within, allowing our entire being to be tampered with, and opening ourselves up to cosmic powers that God never intended for us. As I started discovering more of the truth about yoga and Eastern meditation, I began to realize how truly satanic all of it was.

The devil does not come dressed as an ugly entity. He appears as something beautiful, something that can look and even feel good. He knows what makes mankind tick, and his biggest disguise can look like everything you ever wanted. As I started to dig more, I was finding how compatible chakras, yoga, kundalini, and meditation are with the occult. I remember one day stumbling upon a satanic website where they were practicing opening their chakras. That set off warning bells in my head. What type of spirit was I yoking myself with?

What many don't realize is that the entire spiritual system of yoga is used in Luciferiansm. Yoga constitutes one of the two central pillars in the system of practical and spiritual attainment, encompassed by the law of Thelema. Thelema is an occult philosophy that was taught by Aleister Crowley. It states: *"Do what thou wilt shall be the whole the law."* It is man's will over God's will. Do whatever pleases you while attaining your spirituality within.

"Crowley was among the first to adopt yogic ideas and practices in Western occult context as a means of spiritual attainment on par, or co-terminus, with the Western magical tradition. Crowley viewed the practices and results of yoga as not only leading to high mystical experiences and trances and the development of individual genius but also practical attainments, such as increased will-power, concentration, and self-discipline." (Yoga and the Disenchantment of the West, Frater Aletheia, Thelemicunion.com, 2017.)

This practice became such a pillar in magick, because of the ability to master your mind through concentration. Aleister Crowley was a well-known teacher and author of many occult books. Crowley was the author of the *"Eight Lectures on Yoga,"* which he published in 1939. In this book, Crowley teaches students on the steps of yoga to attain mysticism through several lectures. In the *"Eight lectures of Yoga,"* Crowley explains how to transcend the mind and combine science, magick, and yoga.

According to Crowley, *"Those states of mind which result from the practice of yoga are properly called trances, because they transcend the conditions of normal thought."* (Magick:Liber Aba, Aleister Crowley, Page25.)

Yoga means union. In the *"Eight Lectures of Yoga,"* it is taught, *"The path of yoga is straight with that of magick. It suggests that yoga is the sublimation of philosophy, even as magick is the sublimation of science.... the two flower into these higher states beyond thought, in which the two have become one. And that of course is magick and that of course is yoga."* (Aleister Crowley, Page 51.)

Crowley explains how yoga is magick and magick is yoga. Two streams coming together perfectly as one. Crowley goes on to explain how magick and yoga are *"the cooperation of lovers,"* and that *"yoga is almost essential to success in magick."*

One definition for alchemy is, *"A seemingly magical process of transformation, creation, or combination."* It is a shift in consciousness that returns us from the non-physical to the physical. It becomes clear that the magick rowley is speaking of is none other than alchemy. It is using the asana (posture), pranayama (breath), and the Dharana (concentration) as means to change us mentally and physically.

The word "occult" simply means unseen. Yoga seeks to awaken the occult energies within the body. In all the ancient yoga texts, yoga is described to awaken psychic powers and magical abilities.

All this is why the yoga scholar and Sanskrit authority, Rammurti Mishra, can interpret yoga theory as laying the foundation for occultism. "In conclusion, it may be said that behind every psychic investigation, behind mysticism, occultism, etc., knowingly or unknowingly, the Yoga system is present." (Yoga: The Occult, by Dr. John Weldon, jashow.org)

In Shree Purohit Swami's commentary on Patanjali's Yoga Sutras, he notes, *"In India and Europe, I came across some three hundred people who suffered permanent damage from wrong practice. The doctors on examination could find nothing organically wrong. And because most doctors assume yoga is harmless, they rarely consider its possible relevance to any illnesses of their patients who practice yoga. But we are convinced that many perplexing diseases, including some deaths, are related to yoga."*

According to Richard Kieninger, a New Age educator, *"A woman of my acquaintance upset her hormonal balance doing yoga exercise, and it produced a malfunction in her adrenal glands. She didn't know how to reverse the effects, and soon she died." (Yoga: The Occult, John Weldon, jashow.org.)*

Very serious effects are attributed to yoga practice because *it is not only physical exercise.* It is a mystical practice, and we must not ignore its occult roots. This brings me to my next point: Not only is yoga occult but is seen as the forbidden path of sorcery in Luciferiansm.

Yoga is witchcraft in the truest sense of the word. It is the practice of magic, and magic is the power of influencing the course of events by using mysterious or supernatural forces. This couldn't be any clearer than in the book, *"Liber Hvhi: Magick of the Adversary."* This book is described as *"A grimoire of self-deification, the model of the adversary, the aspects of Samael and his mate, Lillith, how this hidden power within our subconscious may be awakened and brought to fuller potential than previously thought."*

This is what *"Liber Hvhi: Magick of the Adversary"* is all about: awakening from within the very core of New Age thought which is in direct alignment with Satanism. It is the dividing line between becoming a god and the narrow path of Christianity, in which one must die to self as opposed to awakening the divine within and becoming a god. To "awaken the divine" is witchcraft, and that is the serpent power that started in the Garden of Eden. This is what separated us from the one true God.

In the book *Liber Hvhi*, yoga is described as a lone path to Ahriman, which is known as Satan. The book theorizes, *"It is not the worship of Satan but becoming the manifestation of it."* It is described as entering the path of Daeva-yasna.

Daeva-yasna ultimately means "Worship of demons." Let's break it down: The word "Daeva" in Hinduism means, "The divine power itself shining and leading mankind to the Holy path by its divine light."

Whereas, in Zoroastrianism, the word "deva" is derived from the root "dab," which equals, "to deceive." Daeva's are supernatural beings. In other words, they are demons.

The word Yasna literally means "oblation" or "worship." So, when entering this path, using kundalini yoga, you are literally becoming godlike by worshipping yourself and being deceived into thinking the magical abilities you achieve are your own. In

Luciferiansm, kundalini is a big part of Ahrimanic Yoga, also known as, "Encircling darkness by the serpent path."

"Kundalini is considered Lilith, the mother of demons. It is the Sakti that begets all others, she is the desire for continued existence, the very spirit intertwined with Ahriman, her spiritual mate. She is what stirs Ahriman up from his deep slumber, the very fluid motion of creativity and action." (Liber Hvhi: Magick of the Adversary, Michael Ford, Page 110.)

"When seeking to awaken kundalini, you may envision, firstly the black and red serpents within, desire and strength intertwining—both are the form of the adversary within." (Liber Hvhi: Magick of the Adversary, Michael Ford, Page 110.)

Reading what kundalini is to the Satanist is very alarming. The serpent that lies within is nothing more than demonic, and if it's involved in Satanism, then it should have no part in my life as a Christian.

Chakras are another esoteric system that has become very popular. What exactly are these seven energy centers and why would we want them opened? There is no scientific proof that such an energy system exists, and it is thought of more as energy centers that are attached to the nervous system and endocrine glands. In Luciferiansm witchcraft, the seven chakras are fallen angels that lie within.

"There are seven upper chakras, representing the archdaevas empowered, awakened and rise within the mind and the body. There are seven lower chakras representing other chaotic forces which are controlled once the seven uppers are in union within the Yatus. The four hells are connected here as well, three located in the upper chakras, and one located in the lower chakras. Each chakra represents an area of the body and cells, muscles, and nerve centers of those locations... The only union with God you seek is that that begins and ends within." (Liber Hvhi: Magick of the Adversary, Michael Ford, Page 112)

In other words, there is no God but *self,* echoing the same tune as the serpent in the Garden of Eden.

When I first started with yoga and eastern meditation, I would have never imagined the evil that could have been awakened within. I always believed in Jesus, but I didn't know Him. I unknowingly thought I could mesh Him with other beliefs. I opened doors that should have never been opened. I opened myself to spiritual entities that had access to my life, body, and spirit. I immersed myself in occult methods when I dove into the spirituality behind yoga/meditation. I became depressed, anxious, suicidal, and experienced sleep paralysis, as well as demonic visions, and strange energy surges coursing through my body.

There is a wrong and right way to worship God, and that path is a narrow one. This world offers many broad paths and many sensual pleasures. It was so much easier going within and worshipping myself. What I thought was good and peaceful, was selfish and slowly destroying me. I spent years depressed and suicidal, searching for a remedy for my soul. New Age thought, yoga, meditation, self-help never worked. It brought me further down the path of darkness and despair.

Once I reached out to Jesus, I could see that all of the "love" and "light" of New Age was really a mask for pure evil. God shone His light in the darkness.

The Bible teaches this: *(2 Corinthians 11: 14-15) And no wonder! For Satan himself transforms himself into an angel of light. Therefore, it is no great thing if his ministers also transform themselves into ministers of righteousness, whose end will be according to their works.*

It was by the grace of God that I got to see things for what they really were. It has been a very painful journey, one where ignorance has truly been bliss. I've always wanted truth, and Jesus was the truth I was looking for.

Many people are spiritually unaware. I am not here to tell you what to think but to explain what I know and the experiences I have been through that led me to my Savior. My only hope is that you will seek to know who God is and realize not everything that seems good really is. Please pray for God's will and search out the scriptures because we must make the decision of who we are to follow.

(I Corinthians 10:21) You cannot drink the cup of the Lord and the cup of demons; you cannot partake of the Lord's table and of the table of demons.

PART III

MAKING ALL THINGS NEW

CHAPTER 7
DESIRING GOD

(Matthew 7:7)
Ask, and it will be given to you; seek, and you will find;
knock, and it will be opened to you.

My whole life I was seeking, looking for meaning, and searching for truth. I always believed in a Jesus, yet my Jesus was one of my own choosing. If there was a God and there was *truth*, then that truth and that God was an absolute concept, not something relative to what I believed. It was more convenient and exciting to believe in my New-Age concepts and immerse myself in mysticism.

Because of my quest for knowledge and mystery, I was left searching for the divine and had very little use for the Bible. The Bible was boring to me, and I would scoff that it was written by mere men. Sure, there was probably some truth to it, but God was much bigger than that book. In hindsight, I see that the enemy knew my union with New-Age lies would keep me intrigued. While looking for truth, my pursuits would keep me from the only source of real truth… Jesus and the Word of God.

I knew there had to be an answer somewhere. I would often notice nature around me and instantly recognize its intelligent design. I never questioned if there was a God and always knew within my spirit that the creator of the universe was Jesus. It was no mere coincidence that I searched for God; it was the Holy

Spirit all along drawing me in. I think that Satan knew this from the beginning and always tried to lure me elsewhere. Despite his deception, though, God's plan was unfolding in my life.

Throughout the years, something made me hold on to Jesus, but I thought I could intertwine many beliefs. However, real truth was becoming painfully clear to me. I began to question my previous beliefs, and, when I called, Jesus answered. Make no mistake, at first the truth brought much devastation. Having your whole worldview shattered can split your heart in two. I was 34 years old, and I had no idea how to proceed with my life at this point. Darkness and despair threatened to swallow me. For the first time ever, I was faced with the realization that Jesus was a stranger to me. The one I thought I knew was an imposter.

This false Jesus was one that whispered, "Be spiritual, not religious; do not judge; it's going to be okay because you're a good person."

The Jesus I was meeting now was convicting me of sin and showing me darkness that appeared as light. The peace I thought I gained by doing yoga or meditation was counterfeit. I was shown a narrow path, illuminated by Jesus' light. He had outstretched His hand, inviting me to follow Him. I knew there was no turning back to my old life, and I was ready to grab hold of Jesus' hand and travel this path.

My life was changing. I had no idea how to move forward, but I knew that I was ready to surrender. I knew that my primary focus had to be Jesus. In an instant, I knew that everything I had incorporated spiritually in my life was pure deception. The veil over my eyes had been abruptly ripped off. For the first time, I was given real spiritual eyes and could now identify all the darkness that had wanted to consume me.

I found myself completely at the end of my rope. I still suffered from depression and anxiety, but my antidepressants, which I had relied on for so long, were no longer working. In fact, when I went back on them, it had the opposite effect and made me horribly suicidal and feeling out of control. I wasn't sure where to turn. I completely cut out all mystical practices. No more psychics, tarot cards, astrology, meditation, or yoga! My plans of being a health practitioner helping people in mental health was coming to a screeching halt. I was out of plans or ideas for my own life; but I now had Jesus. And little did I understand that my entire life was being demolished only so it could be made new in Christ.

This was a scary time for me because I was giving up control and now, having nothing, learning to lean on the solid foundation of the Lord. Once the shock began to wear off, I picked up a Bible and started to read a bit every day but would often become frustrated due to my lack of understanding. I felt like I was learning an entire new language; I prayed for knowledge. I was desperately seeking to know God and couldn't understand why I still hurt so much. I spent countless nights praying and begging God to help me with the immense pain I still felt.

I was finishing school, raising my kids, battling depression, and now having to live my life another way than I was used to. The anxiety I would feel would take my breath away. I was under so much stress, but no matter how hard it seemed, I still had faith and knew that God was watching over me. In fact, God had always been watching me and waiting for me to say "yes" to following Him. God had always been the quiet voice calling out to me, while Satan would come into my life roaring and steal my focus until I could no longer see. Not anymore. I now had my vision firmly planted on my Savior.

I was beginning a new journey and had been stripped of everything I found comfortable. I was in new territory and found myself fighting a mental battle as well as financial. I was losing everything, including my home. I was also passing college courses by a thin thread. I would often come home from school completely anxious and exhausted. To combat my stress, I would fall to my knees and cry out to God, desperate prayers, begging to know Him, desperate to feel His presence. I would read through the Bible and find comfort in Psalms.

As hard as it was, often while in prayer and reading scripture, there would be moments where my heart would still, my breathing would relax, and a peace would fall over me. I was learning to draw my comfort from a source that the world could never offer. I would read scripture to myself and discover that His word is alive and would soothe my soul like a river. This would be my first step in relying on God and His word. I was being taught that His grace was sufficient in my weakness.

I was ready to start new and follow God. I was ready to attend church and wanted my kids to have a foundation in Christ. I never felt comfortable in church and was nervous about attending. Even though my parents brought me as a kid, I never seemed to understand it and was hostile to the gospel. I felt completely distant in the church I was attending. I still felt like an outsider and as if the church was only going through the motions, but peoples' hearts were far from God.

You go through quite a transformation as a former New Ager. God becomes very real to you when you are saved from the depths of darkness. You have such an appreciation for Jesus, and your heart is surrendered to Him in ways that I'm not sure everyone understands. I found the people at this church to be cold and uninviting.

I had *seen* good and evil with my own eyes and felt out of touch with reality at times. I yearned for God but wanted to experience Him in real, tangible ways. I wanted to share my experiences but felt horrified of how I would be viewed at this church. My soul was parched, and I knew there must be more than simply attending Sunday services.

Having this frame of mind would get me in trouble. I was still looking at spirituality through the lens of a New Ager. I wanted what was beyond this realm. I was looking for God and knew I wouldn't stop until I found Him. Luckily for me, He was closer than I could ever imagine.

Since I felt like this church wasn't for me, I began praying for God's guidance and to send me to a new church, one that was more "spiritual." Well, within weeks I saw an advertisement pop up that seemed like such a fascinating church. They seemed bold and interesting, and—bonus—it was ten minutes from my house.

I happily told my husband about it, and he begrudgingly agreed to try it out. This whole thing had been quite the surprise for him. He watched me completely change my belief system and was trying to be as supportive as possible.

That very next Sunday we arrived in church. It was a small congregation, and we were greeted immediately. People were so loving! I felt welcomed right away. I must admit, besides the welcoming greeting, I wasn't impressed right away but loved the pastor/apostle's style of teaching. It was so passionate, and he spoke with so much conviction.

After service, the pastor, who they referred to as "apostle" came up and introduced himself to my husband and me. I greatly appreciated the warm welcome because in so many churches I had been to previously I felt completely ignored. I could tell my husband already seemed to be connecting to the pastor/apostle. I knew I would try it out again. This church was different than what I had experienced in the past. Although non-denominational, they called themselves a "Five-fold ministry." I wasn't sure what "apostle" meant, but I understood that it was part of the five-fold offices.

As I investigated it, the five-fold ministry was simply a church body consisting of apostle, prophet, pastor, teacher, and evangelist. This is mentioned in the Bible, in Ephesians 4:11. I thought it was cool that this church was taking it back to basics. What I didn't understand was that this was also a church that was under the umbrella of a new movement called the New Apostolic Reformation. We will discuss this movement in a later chapter.

The next day I saw an advertisement at the church for a Friday night flow meeting. It was a prayer meeting that was advertised as, "A no agenda, spirit-led night." We were encouraged to experience the presence of God.

"*Experience*," that's what I wanted. I wanted to encounter God. I longed for His presence. This whole idea intrigued me, and I no longer wanted boring church.

CHAPTER 8
EMBRACE

(Zephaniah 3:17)
The Lord your God in your midst, The Mighty One, will save;
He will rejoice over you with gladness, He will quiet you
with His love, He will rejoice over you with singing.

As I opened the door to the church entryway, I immediately got a sense of mystique and wonder. It was a quiet sanctuary, lights dimmed, and candles adding a soft glow to the room. As I sat down in my seat, I could feel a thick presence fill the sanctuary. Everyone sat praying, while the pastor/apostle stood up front waiting to "flow in the Holy Spirit." He would wait to get a sense, a feeling, or impression from the Holy Spirit about someone in the audience. Many were there to get a word from the Lord or to ask for healing.

A woman sat in the front, next to her son and grandson. It had become evident that the sleeping child she held in her arms was ill, and they were hoping for a miracle. As the pastor/apostle called them to bring the child to the altar, he suddenly stopped and told the grandmother it was her he needed to see. As she made her way up to him, he laid hands on her and told her, "Holy Spirit is telling me you're the one I need to see. There are things going on in your home, activity going on because of your involvement with angels. We are never to worship angels, but God alone." The woman began to cry; what he said to her was true.

I was amazed. I had never met a pastor like this before. This guy must be truly walking with the Holy Spirit. How else could he know such things? He began to place an anointing over her head, and, as she fell to her knees, he told her, "Rest awhile in the Holy Spirit's presence." This intrigued me and drew me in. I always wanted the supernatural, and I felt that I was finally in the right place.

As people were continuing to worship and sit in meditative silence, some people would pray in tongues and speak of visions Jesus was giving them. As I sat in the pew, quietly praying, I felt a thick presence engulf my being, and a very warm sensation around my back, then up my neck. As I continued praying, I felt a force, or energy, rush through my stomach, and I began to feel briefly nauseous. This wasn't like anything I'd previously experienced, and I knew I was in the spirit realm. I hungered for God and was willing to surrender every facet of my being to be near to my Lord Jesus Christ. My heart yearned for truth, and, even within Christianity, I wasn't sure where that line laid. I was determined, nonetheless.

The next thing I knew, the pastor/apostle looked at me in the audience and called me up. He knew I was new and wanted to pray and prophesy over me. As I made my way up to the altar, I became alive with anticipation. What would he have to say to me? The pastor/apostle laid his hands on my shoulders, and, as he stared in my eyes, I saw an otherworldliness. He spoke over me as one who had authority. He did not know anything about me but the words he said were very accurate. I don't think I will ever forget them.

"Daughter, you are a woman small in stature but huge in spirit. You are a woman of justice and truth. Jesus loves you and rejoices that you are His. Jesus has begun revealing things to you, and you do not need to be afraid. Your prayers carry great weight to God, and one day you will be a voice, and many will hear you." Then he prayed I would receive the Holy Spirit, and that my spiritual gifts would be revealed to me.

As I made my way back to my seat, I quietly whispered, "Thank you," to God for His words to me. In that moment, I felt an overwhelming blanket of peace saturate my spirit, a peace that surpasses all understanding. My heart instantly felt flooded with emotion and love overflowing. All of my life I had searched for God, and now I felt He was right in front of me, welcoming me, shining a light in the darkness, breaking my chains of wickedness, and, most of all, running to me.

In that moment, I was a child feeling the embrace of my heavenly Father for the first time. I regretted all the years I followed darkness, chasing a false light that left me empty, terrified, and tormented. I had lived my life in ignorance of God. I had lived for myself, never really caring what God wanted of me. It was easier to follow a New Age religion, where I never had to die to self or worry about the concept of sin. I had been deceived, but God was always there, quietly drawing me to Himself. I was done running from God. I was completely broken, with nowhere else to turn. I knew that night I was ready to follow Jesus and surrender my whole life to Him.

As the prayer service was ending, the pastor/apostle asked if anyone had anything else to say or pray before he closed for the night. Suddenly an older woman stood up and yelled out, "This girl!" She was pointing in my direction. "I have something I must speak to her."

She rushed over to my seat. I was a bit shocked, but she sat beside me and took my hands in hers. Her presence was motherly and, at the same time, comforting. "Honey, the enemy comes around you quite often. He is always whispering in your ear, telling you negative things, trying to destroy you. Know this: You are Christ's and there is now no condemnation for those in Christ Jesus." Then she wrapped her arms around me and hugged me as I broke down crying.

What she spoke to me struck me to the core. My whole life I had followed the enemy through New-Age practices and had often suffered depression and thoughts of suicide. I had often thought that I was oppressed, and my thoughts were not my own. This woman had no idea about my past involvement in the occult, but she was right: The devil had followed me my whole life. Now, it was over. Tonight, was the night God won. I had encountered the presence of Jesus, and I knew my life would never be the same. This prodigal daughter was finally home.

I left that night completely in awe of God. I felt a huge, dark cloud lift from me. I was at the end of my rope, with nowhere else to turn. Sometimes that's exactly where God wants you. A new life was beginning for me, and at last I was at peace with that. I was eternally grateful for the immense love Jesus lavished on me. My heart of stone was softening, and new life was coursing through my veins. My spirit was starting to come alive, the breath of God resuscitating me. I was no longer lost or dying; I was being made a new creation in Christ.

Over the next few weeks I felt different. I felt joyful, and I was madly in love with my Savior. I never understood the term "born again," but that's exactly how I felt. All those years involved in the New Age/occult, left my spirit dying. But now... I walked into new life.

My depression was gone! I honestly never thought I'd see that day. I was no longer on antidepressants, and, prior to this encounter, I was suffering horrible withdrawals. Just like that, it was gone. I still remember the first time I laughed again. It was amazing, and my soul felt free. When you've been depressed for years, sometimes you don't even understand how numb you can become. I forgot what joy even felt like. I had taken true laughter for granted. God had stood with me, and He gave me strength.

When I had left the New Age and gave up yoga, I was terrified and confused. I didn't see the whole picture. I knew Christianity was exclusive at that point, but it was still hard to let go of my beliefs. However, no matter how much it hurt, and no matter how much it looked like my life was falling apart, I still mustered up the tiniest seed of faith. I had surrendered all of it to God, and I promised I'd be courageous even when I was scared.

This would become my first test of faith and a lesson well learned. God met me in a powerful way. He was deconstructing my life while saying, "Follow Me." He had me in the palm of His hand and was in the process of putting all the pieces where they belonged. God had a plan for my life. *What looked destructive was only rebuilding.*

Looking back on my life, I could see God's hand in all I did. I could see the times He called me. There was a reason the enemy tried seducing me from a very young age, but God was relentless in His pursuit of me. I couldn't believe how long it took me to surrender. I could have died so many times—and in many ways I had already died inside—but God had mercy on me and made me whole. It was as if I could drown in a puddle of tears just thinking about how He must love me and how much I didn't deserve it.

After that night, my life did a total 180. Things I used to be interested in now carried very little meaning to me. I was acutely aware of my own actions and how everything I did carried such an impact on others. I remember suddenly meeting strangers and feeling sorrow for them and could instantly recognize the love God had for so many people. I used to be a big drinker; now I no longer craved alcohol.

Another thing that changed, seemingly overnight, was my love for horror movies and darkness. I remember the first time I began to watch a horror flick and the horrible discomfort that came over me. I felt sad, disgusted, and my spirit hurt. This wasn't merely a show I was watching; it was demonic. My new spiritual awareness was overwhelming at times.

Nothing could be more evidence of the Holy Spirit in my life, however, than the absolute love I felt for Christ and my desire to be obedient to His word. I don't think I had ever taken the Bible seriously before, but I now cherished His word and felt real pain thinking about the separation it causes because of our sinful nature. Nothing was worth being apart from God.

In the *1 Timothy 4:1-2*, it speaks of people who follow false spirits and believe lies, people who have turned from truth and had their consciences "seared" as if by a hot iron. Before I encountered God, I never knew how much my conscience had been seared. I did not have the Holy Spirit for guidance and was so blind and hard hearted that I didn't think twice about what was pleasing to God.

In the New Age spirituality, it was always about me. I prided myself on being more spiritual and never religious. I thought I was more awakened, but really my eyes were closed. I was completely oblivious to the immense lies and deception in this world. My idea of a good person was only by the world's standard. The light I sought was darkness, and I had no way of knowing the difference. Only Jesus could be the one to remove the veil over my eyes. Only then could I see the lies and the evil before me.

The Greek word for conscience means to possess "co-knowledge" of something, resulting in one's "sense of guiltiness before God." When we seek knowledge outside of God's word, we are swallowing lies. Soon our conscience loses its ability to sense what is truly right or wrong. We become like hardened criminals with no remorse.

After surrendering to Jesus, however, my heart became soft and my conscience felt everything that would break God's heart. I became keenly aware of how truly guilty I was and how just God would be in His punishment.

The weight of my sin hit me like a ton of bricks. As I sat in a room by myself, praying, I felt the Lord's presence surround me, but this time it felt like conviction. Everything I had done flooded my memory, and I couldn't stop the flow of tears streaming down my face. My conscience had come undone, and I was no longer numb. I thought I had followed God my whole life, but I was really giving myself over to darkness and lies.

Everything I believed in was in direct opposition to God: astrology, numerology, psychics, tarot cards, auras, yoga, Buddhism, and forms of mysticism, all were the enemy of truth. All were forms of the occult and opened doorways to demons in my life. I had lived my life selfishly, but Jesus continued to call me and draw me to Himself. He carried me at my weakest and loved my broken pieces back together. I was torn apart with agony at what I had done and how undeserving I was at this gift of life. How could this God want anything to do with me? I felt ashamed and embarrassed.

I poured my heart out to Jesus and begged for forgiveness. I saw such a stark contrast between the darkness of the human heart and the goodness and mercy of God. I was now a sinner, saved by grace that I could never deserve.

In the quiet, sobering moments that followed between God and me, I realized that no love in this world could ever be greater, and nothing could be worth living for more than Christ. I had found the thing in life that I knew I would live and die for.

CHAPTER 9
SWORD OF THE SPIRIT

(1 John 4:4)
You are of God, little children, and have overcome them,
because He who is in you is greater than he who is in the world.

I sat there in my bed, tears streaming down my face as so much emotion ran through my head. I was brainstorming a testimony to give at church the next day, a speech to represent my public confession of Christ before my baptism. I couldn't wait to be fully immersed as a symbol of dying to myself, being cleansed of my sin, and rising as a new creation in Christ Jesus.

Getting water baptised was an outward expression of the inward change I had already experienced. The Holy Spirit was working within me to seal me with my Savior for the day of redemption. I was no longer a child of the devil, belonging to the world; I was now an adopted daughter of a king. I had surrendered my whole heart to God, and I knew I was now no longer a lost sheep in the world. I was nervous for what this milestone would bring but filled with a heart of gratitude because of the darkness Jesus saved me from.

Life could have turned out very differently for me, but it didn't. I was a recipient of God's grace. At times I felt such sorrow for how I lived my life and how close I was to spiritual death. I walked through life for so long, numb, depressed, and losing the will to live. I had chased "spiritual things" of this world, never knowing the dangerous path I was traveling. Then, Jesus saved me from myself. I didn't earn it, and I didn't deserve it. His love was something the world could never give.

(Psalm 147:3) He heals the brokenhearted and binds up their wounds.

Jesus, all this time, had been searching for me, and yet I was distracted, looking for false peace, looking for the divine within, looking to mystical forms of spirituality while avoiding the Bible and finding out who Jesus was. I was so blind, so hurt. I was a soul that was lost and desperate for a touch of God to quench my spirit from the thirst and hunger I could never satisfy. Because of Jesus, I could see; because of Jesus, I could smile; because of Jesus, I was found; and, because of Jesus, I never had to thirst or hunger again.

I feasted on the Bible daily and earnestly searched for wisdom. I prayed morning and night, and, for the first time ever, was learning about fasting. Fasting became the key that would unlock years of depression I had been through. All those years I was involved in New Age or occult, I had opened doors to my life that I should never have opened. When I began to experience a kundalini awakening, I opened myself up to supernatural powers that were a counterfeit to who God really is. Shortly after giving my life to Jesus, I began reading all I could about fasting and became intrigued.

I remember praying to God about when I should fast, and immediately it was as if He was saying, "Why not now?" So, the next morning I jumped right into it. It was a Sunday, and I spoke to God while getting ready for church, simply telling him, "Lord, please lead me through this fast, and accomplish whatever it is in me that you need to do." I decided I would start by completing my first 24-hour, no-food, only-water fast.

That day I went to church, read my Bible, took care of my kids, and prayed. The hunger pains would come and go, but my excitement to feel closer to God was stronger than anything I felt in my flesh at that time. The day proceeded normally, but I could not have expected what happened that night.

It was late that evening and I had put the kids to sleep, and even my husband was sleeping peacefully. I made my way downstairs with my Bible in hand and quietly sat alone reading scripture and praying to God. I was enjoying this quiet moment between me and my heavenly Father, when I opened to Psalms, chapter 18.

The Lord is my rock, my fortress and my deliverer; my God is my rock, in whom I take refuge, my shield and the horn of my salvation, my stronghold. **(Psalms 18:2.)**

As I read these words, my soul was pierced. The words on that page came alive, and suddenly it was as if I felt the very presence of God fill my living room. I don't think I'll ever find the words to describe the power and holiness that was surrounding me. I felt I could barely stand up. I was filled with absolute awe and an immense reverence for God.

After a few moments, I started to feel anxious, as if a very dark presence entered the room. I finished praying to God and ran upstairs to try to sleep, but when I closed my eyes, I suddenly saw very vivid visions of the most demonic faces. Instead of fear this time, however, I felt the perfect peace of God surround me. I had this knowing that I was being delivered and watching the faces of evil spirits leaving me. I renounced my former activity of all occult practices.

I had suffered from years of anxiety and often insomnia, where I couldn't sleep for days. That night, and every night thereafter, I slept peacefully. The whole next day I could feel the Holy Spirit surround me and keep me in perfect peace. I was filled with immense joy and freedom. I had such deep gratitude, and, at times, wanted to dance. I felt so free. I knew I would remain forever grateful for what the Lord had done for me.

They say your eyes are a window to your soul, and I remember looking into the mirror, and, for the first time, I saw my eyes had a light about them. The color of my eyes looked lighter. They had been darker before. I didn't simply feel different. My whole countenance had changed. I was experiencing many changes in my life, and at times I felt like the luckiest girl alive. It was such a miracle to escape the grips of deception.

It has been said that one of man's greatest accomplishments is seeking God and finding Him. I didn't have everything I wanted in life, but I had the Lord by my side. Because of that, I knew I needed little else. *He* had saved me from darkness, delivered me from evil, and now I would make a beautiful step forward to be baptized in His name.

That day came, and I was ready. I made my way up to the front of the church. Although my voice was shaky, I mustered up the strength to confess what Jesus had done in my life and how I had experienced freedom from depression that only the grace of God could bring. Prior to my own plunge, I watched my two young sons be baptized before me. What a precious sight: my own kids making the decision for themselves that they would follow Jesus.

Next was my turn. As I fell beneath the water and rushed back to the surface, I felt clean and full of joy. Baptism symbolizes a believer's obedience and faith in a crucified, buried, and risen Savior. I now arose from that water a new creation, risen with Christ, ready to begin a new walk, and leaving everything old behind. It was a beautiful day, one where I basked in a cleanliness and a wonderful peace.

Many people there at church came up to me afterwards, hugging me and showering me with love. On our ride home, my 6-year-old son was even overflowing with the newfound love he had found in Jesus. My heart melted as he said to me, "Mom, when I was baptized today, I could feel God holding me!"

I smiled from ear to ear, and said, "Of course He was."

The realization hit me that, yes, Jesus loves my son even more than me, and, as a mother, I could never feel better than to know that my own son rested in the arms of Jesus.

I don't think I could have ever been prepared for what would befall me next. Here I was walking around on cloud nine, feeling elated and enjoying my new life in Christ, only to experience some of my darkest days ahead. After getting baptized, I went through spiritual warfare. That night, I was home after my baptism. I remember feeling suddenly afraid, and a dark presence was looming over me. I was no stranger to this presence, and I knew instantly the devil was mad. There is something about baptism that is threatening to the kingdom of darkness. Everything was going good for me, until this last final step... I was truly blindsided and never saw this coming.

You see, nothing can make the spiritual battle come alive like when you are baptized. It means war! All the spiritual realm had now taken notice of my pledge of loyalty to my risen Savior. And for the ex-New Ager, or occultist, that war was even more intense.

My heart and my commitment were now fully wrapped up in Christ. Prior to this, I was deceived and unknowingly following darkness. I thought I knew Jesus...but Jesus didn't know me. That's what changed. God now claimed me as a child of His own kingdom. He had revealed things to me. He planted my feet firmly in His truth, and now the devil was angry. He lost his grip on me, and, even worse, I was able to expose him. I had the knowledge to now warn others of the trap that lay waiting for them.

I wish I could tell you I was in a place of courage, but I succumbed to fear. I wasn't ready for this dilemma I now faced. Things started going horribly wrong for me, and this was meant as a deterrent from seeking God. At night, I would often feel a dark presence watching me, and, at times, after worshipping God or speaking about Christ, I would be filled with anxiety or feel disoriented. I even developed a fear of being alone. At night I would experience very threatening, menacing dreams. I went through months of feeling afraid and alone, not knowing who I could confide in. I constantly doubted myself and now was keenly aware that I didn't belong to this world anymore.

All of this was a lot for me to take in, and this wasn't simply a mental battle. I was still trying to finish nursing school and raise young kids. I even saw things go wrong in my environment. I was doing clinicals at the hospital, and it was very important for me to do well. I remember having a day where my own energy felt extremely drained. As it happens, the day prior I had prayed and shared Jesus with a suicidal patient.

So, the next day was hell for me. I was given an extremely acute patient load, I was late giving my meds, and all day I had strange people being super rude and derogatory to me. One confused patient even woke up to tell me how useless I was. Already on the verge of tears that day, every computer I was using was freezing on me. That whole day seemed like a nightmare, and there was a steady stream of these kinds of days to come.

God managed to keep me through these difficult days where everything seemed stacked against me. Somehow, things had a way of working themselves out for my benefit because of His grace. But I don't think anything bothered me as much as the day my son told me that, while sleeping in my room, he too experienced sleep paralysis and described being held down. What he described to me sent chills up my spine. He told me of something demonic staring at him. What he described matched exactly what I had a vision of during my kundalini awakening.

My son was super sensitive and had also accepted Jesus the day of our baptisms. I knew he loved God with all his tiny heart. I felt angry; I wanted to protect him; I didn't want him to pay for my involvement in this stuff. Why? Why was this happening? Where was God? I gave Him my life, and now I was scared to even go to Him for fear of being attacked. I didn't understand any of it but sat and prayed with my son, asking for God's protection.

For months I felt like I was in a battle and became spiritually weary. People would suddenly come out of the woodwork and randomly harass me about God or even mock Jesus. I saw the enemy speak to me, through people, many times. It always shocked me. At other times, people would seem to distance themselves from me, without me even having to say much. There is a spirit within people, and when your spirit belongs to the Holy Spirit, it is noticeable to those who don't share that. I became aware of how cold the world could be.

Everything seemed so artificially loving and peaceful within the New Age movement, but Jesus did not tell us we would have unity. Quite the opposite. Jesus said, *"If the world hates you, you know that it hated Me before it hated you. If you were of the world, the world would love its own. Yet because you are not of the world, but I chose you out of the world, therefore the world hates you."* *(John 15:18-19.)*

That verse really started hitting home for me. That was it! Jesus Himself chose me, and, because I no longer belonged to the world, I could not expect to be treated any differently than Jesus Himself. In fact, I came to the realization that if the world did love me, then I probably didn't belong to God because when God chooses you, He sets you apart. Knowing this didn't make life easier, but it did make it worth it. I loved Jesus, and now, knowing the truth, I could never go backwards.

I would often go to prophetic-type worship meetings, and there was one incident that stuck in my head. I remember sitting in the front row, praying, and one of the leaders suddenly said he got a vision. Somehow, I knew this vision described me. This man said he saw, "A vision of a young woman, standing in a dazzling blue dress, and he knew this was God's daughter and she needed prayer. She had a look of fear on her face and the enemy was attacking her. She was holding a big sword, and it was almost too heavy to lift. As she learned to use it, however, it became smaller and quicker and easier to maneuverer.

Somehow, I knew that woman was me. I *was* being attacked and feeling afraid. What that sword described was the Word of God, and, as the leader said, as I learned to use it, it would become my greatest weapon.

I hadn't learned much about the Bible throughout my life, but I certainly didn't know of the power it contained. Scripture is literally God breathed and is alive. At night, I would go to bed afraid but with my Bible right beside me. When I felt oppressed, I would read scripture, pray, and cry. It was in those moments that I could feel a heavy cloud being lifted and darkness moving away from me.

At times, I would get attacked in my dreams but would suddenly wake up speaking scripture, and I would feel peace. The warfare could be intense at times, and I would feel completely drained. The devil seemed relentless. At the time, I was attending a charismatic church, and much of the information I gathered on spiritual warfare was from sources that hyper-spiritualized everything.

It became confusing. There were names for certain spirits and special prayers or books to read. Some sources recommended "binding and loosing." It became repetitive, and I only became more scared and felt as if I was walking on eggshells. But the key to my freedom in Christ did not come from some anointed deliverance minister or special prayer or rituals. Instead, it came from my submission to God.

If only I knew this simple concept. It wasn't easy, but it was simple. We, as humans, tend to overcomplicate things. You see, this was never my battle to fight. The battle was God's. There was nothing, no magic formula I could do, because Jesus already conquered darkness. Any attacks targeting me now were only there by God's permission. I also believe in consequences: I made the decision to follow the darkness of the occult, and now I would be allowed to feel that sting.

Besides that, and most importantly, God was allowing the warfare to strengthen me. God never allows things unless it is serving a purpose that will later bring Him glory. God was allowing this, so I could learn to trust Him. The powers of darkness were no longer masquerading as light, and now they wanted to scare me and dismantle my focus. This was a test. Would I submit to fear or to God?

I had already made my decision, and I would follow God, even when that path looked too hard to trek. I could not lean on my own understanding or strength but had to yield to the power of Jesus. As I read through the chapters of the Bible, all of God's people went through battles that were not their own. Many even argued with God that they were not equipped for what they were called for. The common factor in all was *trust*...to go forward and know that it was going to be God giving the strength.

(Psalm 46:10) *Be still and know that I am God.*

In the New Age, I took this verse out of context and thought it meant for me to be still (meditate) and be my own God. Not so. This verse was speaking of trusting God and not fighting a battle against darkness that belonged to the Lord. Submitting to God required my obedience, knowing the Word of God, and walking in the Spirit. These things would bring the Lord by my side, and the enemy had no place in my life.

Spiritual warfare is common to those who leave the New Age or occult, but this can be such an important time for growth. It is a time for equipping and a time for roots to reach down to good soil. This was all part of the journey to learn to become a disciple of Jesus.

Now, even though spiritual warfare can be commonplace at different periods in the believer's life, it can also be a warning signal that is showing you there is something amiss or a red flag that needs to be noticed. When I was in the New Age, it was God that allowed things to turn ugly, so I could see things for what they truly were. Now, some people in churches experience "spiritual warfare" probably more than they should. For me, it even became a scapegoat. The Lord was showing me what I was allowing in my life was, again, darkness.

The reason I was drawn to the church I was attending was because they practiced the prophetic. Again, I was chasing for signs and wonders, and that can turn into an unhealthy obsession. God would soon teach me that to know Him is to know His son, who is His Word. I would need to have faith, obedience, and the knowledge of the truth. Seeking the supernatural became an insatiable desire that was more about pleasing myself than pleasing God. I became uncomfortable, by God's design, and He carefully placed my feet back on His path of righteousness.

THE NARROW PATH

PART IV

DOCTRINES OF DEMONS

CHAPTER 10
SYNCRETISM

(Jeremiah 23:16)
Do not listen to the words of the prophets who prophesy to you.
They make you worthless; they speak a vision of their own heart,
not from the mouth of the Lord.

As time went on, it became necessary for me to break ties with the church that I was in love with. It began at a typical Friday flow worship night at my church. As always, I looked forward to these unrehearsed, passionate nights to hear from the Lord. I would arrive with anticipation, desperately seeking a touch from the Lord, and to bask in His presence. I loved that my church had real supernatural meetings with the Lord and not only Bible readings. I would anxiously await, hoping to be called up and prophesied over. It felt nice to be 'chosen' and called to the altar, as if God himself had something to speak to me.

I felt slight disappointment that night because I wasn't selected for a special prophetic word. At the end of service, however, the "apostle" told everyone he felt like he needed to do something, and those wanting to could line up in the front of the sanctuary. I quickly rushed forward. As my pastor/apostle lay hands on me, he touched my forehead with oil. He told us the Holy Spirit wanted to give us an anointing. Sometimes when I had hands laid on me, I would feel a little lightheaded. When I looked into the apostle's eyes, there was an otherworldliness there that was almost hypnotizing.

His eyes were a bright blueish/green, and they radiated such peace and spirituality. This man was different than any pastor I had met before. He craved the deeper things of God, and I felt that he was a spiritual superhero that was filled to overflowing with the Holy Spirit.

As I left that night, I felt blissed out and immensely peaceful. Oftentimes, I would come home feeling so spiritually aroused that even my skin would tingle. That night, after being touched on the forehead, I had very vivid visions and had trouble falling asleep. Every time I would close my eyes, I would see visions like on a movie screen. I had convinced myself that I must have some type of prophetic gifting. I would even get excited and want to read my Bible after these "flow in the spirit" meetings, but would end up feeling too intoxicated. Holy Spirit could feel like a drug sometimes, and I felt high.

I experimented with ecstasy in the past, and that's exactly what this felt like. Amazing, I thought, God's presence was a natural high, and all I needed was Him to feel refreshed. I would need little else. I clearly understood that drugs, alcohol, and altered states of consciousness through yoga were merely the counterfeits for God's intoxicating peace.

The Bible did have several warnings about being "sober minded," but I would hear others use the term "drunk in the Spirit" and think that was okay. I needed to feel His presence and bask in His love. Feeling drunk in the Spirit was like being wrapped in His love. It made God real to me and satiated my desire for the supernatural that I always craved.

Everything about this church seemed mystical and exciting. I never knew what to expect. Holy Spirit oversaw the services, and, most of the time, sermons were more focused on the Holy Spirit than even Jesus. Many times, during sermons, the apostle would claim to suddenly get direct revelation from the Holy Spirit and specifically speak to those in the congregation.

Thinking back, I remember one service where my pastor/ apostle, in front of the whole congregation, yelled out with authority to a man and his wife. He spoke on behalf of the "Holy Spirit" and confronted them about what goes on in their private life, also accusing them of speaking wrongly about the pastor/ apostle. Because he was the apostle there, it was accepted that he would hear directly from the Spirit, and, although it made me uncomfortable, I thought he was justified. After all, didn't "apostles" carry greater authority?

The couple didn't deny their supposed behavior, and the apostle, after reprimanding them, had them come to the altar. He gave them his love and require them to apologize and start speaking in tongues to Yahweh.

I had never experienced anything like this at a church, but how quick I was to dismiss it. "What is going on here?" my confused husband leaned over and whispered. I shrugged and said nothing. I mean, after all, this guy did claim to be an apostle chosen by God, and he did know things. However, looking back on this, I can now see this as almost abusive. Even if you were privy to some special information, was it proper to reprimand people in your church in front of the entire congregation?

Well, I would find out later that this was learned behavior. My apostle had a "spiritual father," whom he often spoke about, and he credited his success to him. I had never heard of a spiritual father before, and I attributed this as a type of mentor in his life.

My church was different. I mean, I guess you could say it was a Pentecostal/charismatic church. They believed in spirit baptism and the gifts of the Spirit. But they were considered a 'five-fold' ecclesia. This belief in the five-fold ministry maintains that all five offices mentioned in Ephesians, Chapter 4, are all still operating today.

(Ephesians 4:11) And He Himself gave some *to be* apostles, some prophets, some evangelists, and some pastors and teachers...

The first two mentioned are apostles and prophets, which for so long have not been in the church. My church and many others have started to believe that the church cannot function properly without these two offices being in place. That sounded great to me at the time. This guy must really have it right, I thought. After all, God shows up at this church.

Being new to the faith and an ex-New Ager, I let my feelings lead me. I "felt" God's presence, therefore I willingly accepted what was taught as true. I went to Bible study and didn't question what was taught. Reading scripture is not the same as understanding scripture in context. When someone claims to be an apostle and walks by direct revelation of the Holy Spirit, that is already placing them in a high position and lowering the view of scripture.

So, because the Bible topically lined up with the idea of apostles, I took that verse and, when isolated, believed that there must be these offices today. You couple Biblical illiteracy with supernatural signs and feelings or manifestations, and you have a recipe for deception.

I would soon learn that the Bible is my weapon against deception, and God would lead me out of this church like He had led me out of the New Age.

I was passionate about this church, and almost every Sunday I would feel the tangible presence of God: a thick, weighty presence that would make me almost melt into my chair with peace. To be honest, I loved feeling like this. However, many Sundays, instead of feeling renewed, I felt almost lethargic and too intoxicated to want to do much else, including reading my Bible. Often, the next day I would feel kind of tired and irritable. I couldn't understand why and attributed this to spiritual warfare because of encountering God's presence.

Many times, our church services would end, and people would line up at the altar to have an encounter with the Holy Spirit. My pastor/apostle would prophesy over people, and it was common to see people "slain in the Spirit." This is when, after getting touched by the pastor/apostle on the forehead, people would fall back and lose consciousness for several minutes. It was during this floor time that they were having healing work done to them by the Holy Spirit. There were times I wished to come under the power of the Holy Spirit so powerfully that I would fall back as well. This never did occur for me, and I believe this was God's protection.

Just coming out of the New Age, I still had much of the same mind. I craved the supernatural and would look forward to each church service with anticipation so that I could feel the presence of God move. I know without a shadow of a doubt that the Lord was with me, and I had become a changed person; however, I became obsessed with this church and saw the apostle of this church as truly anointed. I began thinking how I could never leave this church, and the thought alone would frighten me.

The spirit in this church had a hold on me. I believed we were all meant to be at this church, and, in hindsight, it felt almost like being under a spell. It had a very mystical quality to it and was very sensual, although at the time I viewed it as super spiritual and looked down at other churches as dry and devoid of the Spirit of God.

This pastor/apostle was full of passion and zeal for the Lord and was good at eliciting an emotional response from his congregation. He was very guru-like, and people looked up to him. I started looking into the book he had written about his journey with God. That's where I learned a little about his background.

My pastor/apostle had written a couple of books, and one was about fasting. He had completed quite a few fasts, and a couple of them were forty-day fasts. He used to be an Assemblies of God preacher but ended up falling into sin and having an extramarital affair. This led him into a downward spiral and away from God for many years.

When he came back to God, there was a certain man, another apostle, who he considered his "spiritual father." This man owned a church in Panama City, Florida. He had gone back to see him and describes confessing his sins to this man. This apostle then told him that his sins were forgiven. It was then that he had a supernatural experience of something 'reverberating' in his entire being, and the weight of shame and guilt leaving him out of the top of his head.

After this experience, he was instructed to preach again. Reportedly, as he was writing a sermon, the Holy Spirit spoke to him and told him to stop preparing his message. Instead, he perceived the Lord speaking to him that, "God would put His words in his mouth, and he would become an oracle." At first, I was amazed at this. This guy was hearing from the Holy Spirit, audibly! I wanted that type of relationship with God as well.

The pastor/apostle of this church attributes a great anointing being transferred to him because of lengthy fasting and his spiritual father. I began wondering about the word "apostle." After all, this is what my pastor called himself. He would talk about this often, and, as a new believer, it sounded like an amazing story. After he completed one of his forty-day fasts, after being alone in a room with only him and God, he audibly heard the Holy Spirit speak to him. When he had taken this fast, his wife had left him, and he wanted God to reconcile his marriage.

When the Holy Spirit spoke to him, he said, "Okay, son, what do you want? Me or her?"

The pastor/apostle wanted to be God's "man," so he chose to chase God, and let his marriage end. The next thing he heard was "the Spirit" tell him he was to be His "apostle" and go forth and start his own church.

Now, at the time, I believed all of this. I mean, I never for one second thought he was lying. I knew how sincere this guy was. I also knew from my own experiences how powerful fasting can be. It does open you up to the spiritual realm. So I never doubted this and believed that my pastor/apostle was super spiritual, as was I, and that was part of the draw to this church. Engaging the supernatural was exactly what I wanted.

As time went on, though, I couldn't help but wonder if my pastor/apostle "tested the spirits," as the scriptures warn in *1 John 4:1-6*. One thing I knew from New Age was that people always seemed to receive channelled messages by some audible voice. Can we always trust that whatever voice we hear is from God? This began to nag at my spirit, but I ignored it. His sermons were always fiery and sounded Biblical. I saw what I thought was the power of God displayed at this church, so his experience had to be from God. After all, the Bible speaks of apostles as one of the five offices, so why couldn't that exist now?

I didn't know much about the Bible as a baby Christian and thought taking isolated scriptures would be okay. However, scripture must interpret scripture and context is everything.

This became a very confusing time for me. Trying to piece together all I had experienced up until this point had been very difficult. I experienced plenty of supernatural happenings and spiritual warfare. I also had *so* many questions and was desperately trying to find my way to the truth. This church was very big on signs and wonders and activating your spiritual gifts. Many spoke in tongues. I became obsessed with the prophetic and wanted to receive all the gifts I could from God.

At the time, I thought this was super spiritual and simply me wanting to serve God, but honestly it was more carnal. Constantly seeking after a sign was equated with adultery.

Jesus said to those who asked him for a sign, *"An evil and adulterous generation seeks after a sign. (**Mathew 12:39**.)*

"Adulterous" refers to seeking something outside of God. It is sensual and seeking after signs doesn't require faith.

During our Friday flow worship time, the environment was set up to move the emotions. Lights were dimmed, repetitive music was played, and meditative-type silence was used to usher in the presence of the Holy Spirit. People, during this time of prolonged prayer and seeking God in worship, would often describe visions, speak in tongues, and various people would prophecy—although most of the focus was on the pastor/apostle to "flow in the Spirit" and speak what was given to him.

To me, these became a time of refreshing, and I had simply traded my Eastern style meditation for basking in the presence of the Holy Spirit for my relaxation. What I didn't understand at the time was how this was the same as contemplative prayer, or a new practice called "soaking." The purpose of contemplative prayer was to clear one's mind while repeating a word or song. The goal was to feel God's presence and listen for guidance from Him.

Soaking prayer is like contemplative prayer, but it usually includes worship songs and sitting or lying for prolonged periods of time, waiting to feel certain spiritual manifestations from God. During these times, I would anxiously wait for the presence of God to fill the room. Eventually, I would feel an immense peace and often a burning or warmth that would start to crawl up my skin. Afterwards, I would feel tingling on my skin and euphoria for some time afterwards.

I began to crave this feeling and loved how all my troubles seemed to melt away. I needed to feel God's presence and chased this high. I also searched for supernatural gifts and read all kinds of prophetic books. I thought I was searching for the deeper things of God, when I was really seeking more of myself. I truly loved Jesus, but I was engaged in very mystical practices, however well-meaning I was.

This soaking-type prayer was not Biblical Christianity, but mysticism. The very definition of mysticism is, for one, "Belief that union with or absorption into the deity or the absolute, or spiritual apprehension of knowledge inaccessible to the intellect, may be attained through contemplation and self-surrender"; and two, "Belief characterized by self-delusion or dreamy confusion of thought, especially when based on the assumption of occult qualities or mysterious agencies."

By the very definition, mysticism is defined by occult practices. It is more often thought of as "religious ecstasies" and transformations.

I always thought of myself as a Christian mystic, and I couldn't see anything wrong at the time. I craved that ultimate union with God. In fact, I remember the evenings of prayer at my church and feeling an overwhelming presence of the Holy Spirit. The suggestive mood was set as usual, beautiful melodies filled the air, and we all sang the same chorus beautifully, ushering in the most wonderful presence.

Such peace… It was as if my entire being started to electrify with surges within me. A sudden rush of hot embers prickled throughout my skin, up my shoulder blades, neck, and head. Pure bliss.

The apostle suddenly stood up and, with great anticipation, announced, "*He's* here…the smell of baking bread, I can smell Him. It's the Holy Spirit! If anybody here has prayer requests, now is the time to ask God. Our sound has reached to the heavens!"

One woman went and lay on the floor, giving God reverence, while another woman, a prophetess, could barely stand up, saying she was "a bit drunk in the Spirit."

I sat there feeling drunk myself and thanking God He was there, as I sat and prayed for all His wonderful spiritual gifts. I was told we are to "earnestly desire the spiritual gifts," and I did!

As I walked out of church that night, I felt a total state of bliss. At times I really did feel like I was having a spiritual awakening. I noticed the trees, the sky, and colors appeared more vibrant to me. I would go places, meet people, and feel such a sense of love for that person standing in front of me—almost moved to tears. I felt extremely sensitive to what I thought were energies and loved the amount of empathy I felt. Nagging at the back of my mind, however, was the memory of feeling enlightened in the New Age. This couldn't be same thing; right? I concluded that it wasn't.

As I arrived home after the Friday worship session, I sat on my couch feeling so high I probably could have floated to the ceiling. I had intentions of studying God's word when I got home, but, like many times before, I found it hard to concentrate in the daze I was in. Any time I closed my eyes, visions would come, and sometimes I would see colors too.

Being in this mystical state, I sat on my couch and prayed for tongues. Many in my church spoke in tongues, and I wanted to claim this supernatural gift for myself. I thought speaking in tongues would unlock mysteries and give power and access to other gifts. So, I sat there, trying to speak and ask the Holy Spirit to take over my language.

I sat there for several minutes, babbling away, when I suddenly felt a power go through my chest and up my throat. It felt like my tongue was taken over. Words flowed effortlessly out of my mouth. This was it, I thought, God had given me supernatural tongues. I felt such a rush of adrenaline and peace course through my being. I had been told at church that tongues were for edification, and I felt amazing after this experience—at first.

I kept trying to speak in tongues that night and eventually grew tired and went to bed. As I woke up the next morning, I couldn't wait to spend time with God and practice my new prayer language. I made my coffee, grabbed my Bible, and sat down to read. No sooner did I flip open my Bible, than I felt like I got slammed by an immense, sinister energy. I felt instantly irritable, emotional, and like my head was in a severe fog. I couldn't think straight, and my thoughts were racing. What was going on? This was a complete 180-degree turn from all the bliss I felt the night before. My body felt heavy, and a complete emptiness arose against me.

The whole day seemed chaotic for me, and my youngest son started to act out aggressively. This felt like complete oppression, and I knew this feeling from my dabbling in the occult. Confusion set in. Why was I feeling like this? Oh, I know I had convinced myself this was spiritual warfare. Because I had encountered God in such a powerful way, the forces of darkness were mad, so they were attacking me. This would become a repeated theme for me: experience God's presence, then get spiritually attacked. That left me looking for spiritual warfare tactics and reading about deliverance ministries, none of which seemed to help

For forty-eight hours after this experience, I felt depressed and oppressed. The next day was Sunday. I went to church and felt awful there. Everyone was experiencing this move of God and being emotionally moved. For the first time, I sat there and felt nothing... What was going on? I'm always sensitive to the Spirit, I thought to myself. "Oh, Lord, what have I done?" I said from within. The Holy Spirit won't even come around me.

I went up to the altar after service and had the pastor/apostle pray over me, but I couldn't get any peace from whatever was dragging me down. That night, at home, I fell to my knees and prayed. I prayed about this awful darkness that now surrounded me. Was this a punishment for speaking in tongues? I started reading articles online, and what I found struck me to the core. The way I tried to speak in tongues was by simply repeating syllables or even saying words and letting "the Spirit" take over. What I had come across was dozens of testimonies about people trying to acquire the gift of tongues in this way and having another spirit take over. Some people would be praying in tongues in church and a visitor would be at church, understand the language, and say that person was blaspheming God.

While reading some of these testimonies, I immediately felt such a great conviction wash over me. I instantly knew what I was seeking and that it was wrong—very wrong. I will never forget the sorrow I felt that night. My heart cried out to God with such repentance, begging for mercy. Suddenly I knew… God was letting evil spirits attack me because God corrects His children.

Still, I felt very depressed for the entire next day. I ended up reaching out to a Christian friend of mine and begging her for prayer. That night, as I sat trying to read my Bible, I felt an amazing sense of peace wash over me, and in an instant the darkness left me. I called my friend the next day and asked her if she had in fact prayed for me. She had, while working at a prayer call center. Many were praying for me at the exact moment I felt the Holy Spirit surround me. I was immensely grateful and became more cautious and aware of my emotions.

I'll admit, this became a constant battle within. I warred between thinking I was being attacked for engaging in mystical practices and wondering if the enemy was trying to scare me from seeking the deeper things of God. I badly wanted to believe the latter.

As time went on, I began to question the atmosphere that went on in these worship meetings. After this tongues experience and praying for answers everywhere I went, I kept seeing the Bible verse about testing the spirits.

(1 John 4:1) Beloved, do not believe every spirit, but test the spirits, whether they are of God; because many false prophets have gone out into the world.

Even while driving home from school one day I was bombarded with the same theme. I turned on the radio, and it happened to be a show about testing the spirits. When I questioned my pastor/apostle about this, I felt brushed off and was told that verse was meant for something different.

The lack of discernment or testing of anything really began to nag at me. Coming from the New Age, I knew you couldn't believe everything supernatural was from God. The constant working up of an atmosphere, to me, seemed much like conjuring up a presence. How was it that the pastor/apostle could always guarantee that it was Jesus who showed up?

Then there was the prophesying. Being from the New Age, I wanted to know the difference between a prophet and a psychic. Could they be the same? It started to make me feel uncomfortable.

Was the Holy Spirit a force, an energy, like the auras we sought in the New Age? Or was He an actual person, a member of the Godhead? Was the Holy Spirit someone you could command at will?

I loved the people at this church, and the thought of leaving was too much to bear. It became a rollercoaster ride for me. One day I was high on the Holy Spirit, the next day I was miserable and felt irritated. Still, at other times, I would feel such a God connection, then I'd try to read the Bible and my mind would become assaulted with the most blasphemous thoughts. I knew these thoughts did not originate from me and was very taken back and became fearful. There were very strange things that happened from my connection to this church, but I always brushed it off because I had convinced myself I was meant to be there.

The warning signs heightened one day when I mentioned the church to my dad. I was excitedly telling him about this Holy Spirit-filled man that was my new pastor/apostle. He looked at me, interested, and said, "Oh, yeah! What's his name?"

When I told him, his eyes widened. My father knew this pastor/apostle. In fact, this was the same man that had my father come up to the altar, way back when my dad was an alcoholic. He told me how the pastor/apostle had lightly touched him on the forehead, and he'd fallen, slain in the Spirit. He woke up speaking in tongues.

This was amazing, I thought! It had to be meant to be. God saved my father through this man, and now He saved the daughter.

However, my dad would go on to describe, after this supernatural experience, that he too would have very blasphemous thoughts. This must be part of the battle, I thought; you know, the devil was just attacking you. It was spiritual warfare.

Now, as I have mentioned before, a huge turning point for me was when I read Johanna Michaelson's, *"The Beautiful Side of Evil,"* when I was entrenched in the New Age. I still followed this woman's ministry, and again she would become an integral part of my life. I would see, on her ministry page, posts about NAR (New Apostolic Reformation). This was a new movement in the church. Its followers believed that God was bringing back the offices of apostle and prophet. It was also a prophetic movement that encouraged signs, wonders, and Christians being able to perform miracles.

Well, my pastor called himself "apostle"; but he was the real deal, I thought. Maybe some of those churches were steeped in deception, but not my church, I tried to convince myself. I hated what Johanna Michaelson had to say. I respected her for her knowledge on the occult, but even though she came out of the occult doesn't make her an expert on Christianity. Still, the more things I saw on this topic, the more I saw red flags.

I would watch some well-known churches, such as Bethel, in Redding, California, and immediately get a check in my spirit. The strange manifestations people would be exhibiting appeared very demonic to me. The more I researched similar churches, the more I wanted to stay far away from churches like that.

I would argue with myself that my church didn't have the same kind of strange manifestations: no creepy "holy laughter," or convulsions on the floor. Most of what I experienced at my church was positive, and I would ignore anything strange as part of being engaged in the supernatural. I didn't want to give up the powerful experience of God's presence, and I loved our once-a-month communion night. They were special and sacred, and I always felt moved by the Spirit.

Jesus had become my life, and I always wanted to connect with Him, often seeking solitude to have quiet time with God. I fasted often, sometimes for one day, sometimes three, and a few times I did a 21-day Daniel fast. I will admit I did these fasts usually to try to seek God and to experience supernatural phenomenon. I would often get very vivid dreams.

I felt like I was becoming more spiritually awakened and found it strange that I started experiencing weird, cold sensations traveling through my body. This was alarming to me, since this was a supernatural-awakening symptom that happens from kundalini.

There was a book I reached for by a man named Andrew Strom. He was a charismatic pastor who had been involved with this NAR movement. He wrote a book titled, *"Kundalini Warning: Are False Spirits Invading the Church?"* What I read in this book was very eye opening. There were so many similarities to what I experienced in church and what I encountered in kundalini cults, I really was shocked. But in Strom's book he mentions many in these movements having snake dreams and warning dreams prior to their ministries being imparted with a false spirit.

In 2009, Mike Bickle reported a very disturbing dream which he published on the IHOP website. *"I had a long prophetic dream... I finished preaching after the second session about 5:00 PM. Demonic principalities were being cast to earth. They looked like large snakes and heads of a dragon. Many were descending from the sky down to earth. These snake-like principalities were filled with rage against the people. All the leaders and people in various charismatic streams ran in fear and confusion."* (Kundalini Warning Page 58.)

He goes on to describe these snakes biting people.

Another dream that was written in Andrew Strom's book was by a woman who was involved in the Toronto Blessing, in 2000:

"I had a vivid dream of a huge python that came through the back door and attached to my car and rooms of my house. I was very disturbed and sought the Lord for answers." (Kundalini Warning: Are False Spirits Invading the Church, Andrew Strom, Page 24.)

I had a meeting with my pastor/apostle when I first got saved, and I told him my story of leaving the New Age. We had an interesting conversation, and I remember him telling me of a dream he had. He was talking about a prophetic snake dream. In this dream, he described a huge, black python-type snake that was actually very beautiful. He told me this snake was symbolic of breaking down the "spirit of religion." He spoke of people having religious spirits. He felt God wanted to break down these walls and create people that could go out and do things with authority.

This sounded great to me. I used to hate the word "religion" and liked this new emphasis on relationship. It all seemed exciting to me. Little did I know, however, what type of connection would be made from this python dream. Then my eleven-year-old son started having repeated dreams about these snakes. It is a fact that people experiencing kundalini awakenings often have snake dreams. I don't think this is coincidence.

Given the fact that the manifestations going on in churches today mimic kundalini awakening symptoms, I must admit that this makes me very uncomfortable. It was one of those things I kept in the back of my mind. Many things I read in Andrew Strom's book were very hard to ignore. I knew exactly what kundalini looked like and was very wary and shocked that the same thing could have entered the church.

Even though I had several red flags going on around me, I could not and I would not acknowledge that maybe somewhere along the line I could be involved in deception again. I was already saved from New Age lies and freed from years of depression. I experienced many supernatural occurrences at this church, and being close to God made me feel special and anointed.

I felt like I had a very rich, devoted life to Christ: I longed to feel God's presence, I prayed often, I read my Bible every day, and I regularly fasted. Jesus was my first and foremost. I loved the Lord and surrendered my all after leaving behind the occult and New Age. I had been through much spiritual warfare and was very serious about my new life in Christ. I wanted to do everything I could to live for Him.

God knew my heart but so did Satan; and I was about to endure even further testing.

I had spent the month doing a Daniel fast and going through several periods of what I thought was spiritual warfare. I had the strange tongues experience, blasphemous thoughts, and some real spiritual highs and lows. I'll admit I was confused, but confusion doesn't come from the Lord.

During this period of my life, I had come to love worship music, and some of the newest songs were very beautiful and could powerfully move the emotions. One day, I had the most powerful supernatural experience I could have ever dreamed of while I was in my car, driving to class. I had been feeling low, just finished fasting, and was very worn out.

I started out praying in my car, as usual. I was praying and seeking God for answers; I asked for His forgiveness and promised that, no matter what, I would trust Him; I apologized for doubting about this church and began to sing my heart out to a song by Elevation Worship. I had tears streaming down my face and really was moved in worship, when, suddenly, the atmosphere began to change.

I will never be able to fully describe the atmosphere that surrounded me. It felt like a warmth started to slowly intensify and swirl around me. Imagine golden, liquid love being poured throughout your entire being, igniting a passionate fire, and its flames burning, consuming, and climbing up your body until whatever it was bloomed into complete and utter ecstasy.

This probably went on for about ten minutes but was so intense I felt like my heart could possibly burst because my flesh could not handle this intensity. I remember, at one point, sobbing uncontrollably and thanking God for striking me with His fiery presence. I felt like I had tasted heaven, and it was pure bliss. All my troubles and questions melted away. I thought to myself,

"God is rewarding me for my faithfulness, He is showering me with His pure love." The "fire of God": this was what charismatics talked about. Holy Spirit was equated with fire, and so I thought *feeling* His manifested presence, as such, was what it was all about.

After this intense experience dissipated, I found it hard to function the rest of the day. I tried going to class and was overcome with these immense feelings of love for others and had trouble not being a slobbering, crying mess. I was radiating so much love for everyone I encountered.

My high was starting to crash downward, when suddenly I felt a feeling of terror and panic, for absolutely no reason. I texted my pastor/apostle on the way home and told him of my mystical encounter. He rejoiced with me, and this fed into my delusion of being anointed by God. It made me feel super exalted and special. I felt like God had literally poured heaven down on me.

Later that night, however, at home, I felt horrible! I felt very tired, irritable, and afraid. The presence I felt around me that night was sheer terror, and again I fell asleep crying, wondering why I was being attacked. I prayed that night and read scripture, which seemed to sooth my aching soul.

I had to leave school and was starting to feel extremely lethargic. I would often question this fire experience and couldn't bring myself to believe that I could have been tempted so severely. How could God allow such deception, if that's what this was? Truth is, I felt completely drained after this experience, but the high was worth it. It made me feel so close to God. This is exactly what I was seeking after.

I never quite had peace about this experience, and, if I'm totally honest, what I felt was exactly like a full-blown kundalini experience. Often, kundalini can be described as complete bliss and then turn very terrifying. I wasn't ready to accept this. I couldn't wrap my mind around seeking God and getting duped.

During all of this, I was in the process of writing this book. I was so happy to be saved and so enthralled with the mystical that my book was going to be about my journey from New Age to Christianity. Then I would tell about the transition to charismatic

Christianity and the presence of the Holy Spirit. I was beginning to completely fall for this New Apostolic Reformation.

I was at my church for about a year, and, over the summer, we had received an announcement that a prophet would be visiting our church. This prophet was the grandson of my pastor/apostle's spiritual father and had travelled to our church, courtesy of this other apostle. There was a lot of emphasis on this man coming, and it seemed like something many were very excited for. I was intrigued and curious as to what this experience would be like.

The night of his arrival was on a weeknight. My Pastor was filled with amazement that he was there, sharing space with us, and the evening was ripe with anticipation. He was a young prophet, probably in his 20's, and he was really into music and playing the guitar. He was kind of like a musical prophet.

After a little meet and greet, we all made our way to the sanctuary. There I anxiously sat with my husband and my six-year-old son. This prophet began by chanting in tongues and then became somewhat musical and poetic in what he had to say. He sat there saying a whole lot about nothing. He was very loud and passionate. What caught my attention more than anything was the New Age language he proceeded to use. He specifically called God, "source." He made a lot of references about Jesus being seated at the right hand of the Father and alluded to us being able to carry the same anointing as Jesus. I was very uncomfortable with referring to God as "source." This was very common in the New Age, and I was immediately bothered in my spirit.

He was saying very creative things and seemed to want to hype the congregation up to do church differently. He kept saying things like, "No more boring church," and "God is building a frequency, and a 'vibration' for Him to ride in on." There was a lot of emphasis on the secret place but very little emphasis on the Word of God. He was promising people a relationship with Holy Spirit they never had before.

It wasn't long before the whole room was filled with what they were saying was the "Holy Spirit." The presence I felt, though, was one that was heavy, weighty, and very oppressive. I immediately started to feel immense panic and a sense of dread. In that exact moment, my son turns to me with fear in his eyes, shrugging on my shoulder, "Mom, there's something really wrong here!"

I was shocked! "What are you talking about?" I said back to him.

He couldn't put into words why, but he was visibly anxious. I quieted him down but was amazed he must have felt the exact same dread I was feeling. This was such a strong presence that, as much as I tried to resist, it overcame me, and, at times, I felt sick to my stomach. As I looked over at everyone in the congregation, people looked like they were under a spell and almost idolizing this man.

This man was speaking of a new movement of apostles and prophets and us taking over the earth. There was much talk of "channels" and "portals" and "frequencies." As new as I was to the faith, I knew in my spirit this was wrong, and this was occultic teaching.

At the end of service, this prophet laid hands on people and prophesied. I refused to have hands laid on me. I found it curious that my pastor/apostle was encouraging us to really "connect" with this man and touch him, try to absorb his anointing. He wanted us to be imparted with this spirit.

I left that night feeling very alarmed and confused at what I had experienced. At home, I started having tingling all over my body and was even a bit hypersexualized. Why was I suddenly feeling like this, as if I was on a drug or something? Whatever I was feeling was very familiar to me. I instantly knew this was a kundalini spirit. It was the same. I had felt this way before, and I was shocked.

The next morning, I felt horrible! I was so tired, I could barely move, and I was very irritable and angry for no reason. What was wrong with me? What I experienced the night before was not something I could forget. Who was this this so-called prophet? As I started looking into him, I realized he was a real Bethel Church enthusiast. I was starting to realize how big and connected this prophetic NAR movement was.

One thing that really startled me was this prophet's interest in a woman named Annalee Skarin. She was an author and wrote a well-known book, called, "Ye are Gods." Annalee Skarin was a member of the LDS (Latter-day Saints, or Mormon) church. When she wrote this book, "*Ye are Gods*," the content had her ex-communicated.

"*Annalee believed fervently in the LDS doctrine of physical translation. She believed she could achieve this state by perfecting self in Christian principles such as love, faith, and gratitude. She also practiced a meditation technique that she referred to as "thought control." (Annalee Skarin, Wikipedia.org.)*

She believed this meditation technique in which anyone could translate themselves directly to heaven. Annalee was known as a Mormon mystic, and many of her writings had a New Age flair. My heart sank. If you are a so-called prophet, you shouldn't be taking your theology from a woman who is teaching New-Age principles, whose writings are featured among Mormons. This was not Biblical Christianity.

The wheels in my mind were turning. I was so disturbed; the nagging in my spirit wouldn't quit. About a week later, after this "prophet" showed up, I met up with a friend from church, and I unleashed all my concerns on her. She wasn't at church the night that this happened and understood my concerns.

The next morning, I received a phone call from my friend. She was quite the dreamer and told me about a dream she had. After we had talked, she had a vivid dream about our conversation. As we spoke about the prophet in the dream, she suddenly saw the word "cult" written, and someone scream out the word. She was very upset about this dream.

Oddly enough, I started researching that same day about this man in Florida who was my pastor/apostle's spiritual father. To my surprise, one of the first things I pulled up online about this man was a website about him entitled, "Charismatic Cult Leader." What I found was a website that had videos posted of my pastor/apostle's spiritual father, who exhibits authoritarian abuse, tells his congregants that their salvation depends on sticking with him, that he is not a disciple of Christ but a "chief apostle," and that he is even a better apostle than Paul.

Most shockingly, this man tells his congregation, *"I'm all for learning the Bible, but let's read it and then move on. God didn't send us a book, He sent us the Holy Ghost."* This apostle is the head of a church in Panama City Florida and has sent out other "sons" and "daughters," to start churches, under the banner of "The Rock Churches," in many different locations.

There are also videos of this man exhibiting controlling and spiritually abusive tactics, even expecting his congregation to pay off his $800.000 home. When they came up short for the amount, his congregation was rebuked. I also came across two more blogs by people that had left other Rock churches started by this man. They were all being accused of spiritual abuse and teaching unbiblical doctrine. Instead of preaching the Gospel, these types of churches are preaching something known as "The Gospel of the Kingdom." We will discuss this later.

Another thing I found strange was that this head apostle, my pastor/apostle's spiritual father, kept many of his sermons private. You needed a passcode to watch any sermons online. I strongly suspected that was because he was aware that the people who viewed his videos online could call him out. Those who have nothing to hide, however, hide nothing. I was very upset at these findings and highly angered.

What I didn't understand was my pastor/apostle, who really did not seem cult like. In fact, everybody at my church seemed loving. Again, I chalked this up to my pastor/apostle having poor discernment. Maybe he didn't see or know some of the things his spiritual father said.

So, I still chose to stay at this church, for probably another year. I had convinced myself that my pastor/apostle was not anything like his spiritual father, and this prophet was not a normal part of our church. So, I concluded he was a visitor, and maybe I was overreacting. However, as time went on, I began to have demonic nightmares and scary visions again. Now, the only time I had frightening visions was when I was involved in yoga/

meditation, and it was after kundalini awakening. Why was this happening again? I thought I was free from this!

It was that quiet voice within, telling me something wasn't right. If this only happened from opening occult doors in the past, that same thing must be happening again. "That's it," I thought. I couldn't take the nagging in my spirit. Something was very wrong. I needed to fully surrender this to God.

The most frightening thought was the thought that "I'm writing a book; not just any book, but a book about God." That was essentially teaching. I had the power, through my writing, to influence people for the better or for the worse. I would be held accountable for every word I spoke. I needed to know truth.

I got down on my knees and cried out to God, "Lord, I seek the truth because I know you *are* the truth. I'm scared, and something isn't right here. If I need to leave this church, then so be it. Please, I'm begging you, give me the truth of this situation, even if it destroys me!"

Again, my prayer, seeking the truth, would turn my world upside down. About a month after saying this prayer, that same prophet guy was being welcomed back to our church. I was very upset about it but decided to fast and pray about this situation. The night before the service, I had been water fasting and spending a lot of time in prayer, asking God to lead me. That night, I went to sleep and had a very vivid dream. In my dream, I was in my church and this prophet was there, standing in the pulpit. I remember looking at everyone's faces, and they looked extremely lost and confused. They were sheep without a shepherd. I felt immense sadness looking at all the lost faces.

Then I could see this strange energy emanating from the prophet, and it fell on the people like a blanket of darkness. This was a spiritual blanket, and it was demonic. I woke up knowing that this dream was not coincidental. It was very clear. I want to mention here that I had had dreams in the past where I was in his church and it was filled with spirits, however, I never paid close attention until now.

The following morning, I went to this service, where the prophet was speaking. Before he started talking, my pastor/apostle got up and announced that the Holy Spirit revealed to him that this prophet was "only amongst three prophets that Yahweh had released in the land today." I found that to be a very bold statement. There was no fear displayed for speaking for God. It was starting to become clear to me what a delusion this all was.

As I watched this prophet preach, he again was speaking about frequencies and other New-Age type doctrine. It was all about "Kingdom Now" and becoming one with God. There was a lot of emotionalism and getting people hyped up and excited to do church differently.

What was not mentioned was the name of Jesus or God's word. He told people to let their guard down and enter the "presence." He also said religious spirits must go, that Yeshua wasn't going to accept it.

The doctrine of "dominionism" was being preached. This was not normal eschatology from the Bible. This was a false doctrine that teaches that we must take over the earth with the seven spheres of influence (religion, family, education, government, media, arts and entertainment, and business) and that God is waiting for us to subdue the earth before He can come back. Later, in another chapter, we will be covering this doctrine and how it relates to the oneness agenda and different spheres of occult writings.

As I left that day, I finally vowed to never return. I wish I could say to you that I immediately had peace about this decision, but I didn't. The days afterward were filled with agony, confusion, and deep sorrow. I had already left years of the occult and New Age and had my whole perception changed, only to be swept up in a whirlwind of emotionalism and seduction in Christianity. I missed my church family, I missed God's presence, I missed what I thought was a supernatural work of the Spirit.

There is no pain like spiritual pain. To feel deceived again, when all I wanted was to reach up to God, broke my spirit like nothing I had ever experienced. I grew cold and bitter. This almost destroyed my faith. I was angry at God. "How could you do this to me, when all I wanted was to know you?"

I plummeted into very dark despair. If I thought I had experienced spiritual warfare before, I hadn't seen anything yet. I was so depressed I could barely function, and a constant barrage of negative thinking assaulted me. "You are wrong; God is angry at you; you left a true church of God, and that's why you're hurting; the Holy Spirit has left you." These are the lies the enemy whispered in my ears.

I was even struggling with anxiety. I started to believe some of these statements because God had never been quieter. I thought I was doing the right thing, but why did this hurt so bad? There were so many thoughts running through my head. On top of it, I felt convicted to contact the pastor/apostle and tell him why I left. I was terrified.

Eventually, with tears streaming down my face, I wrote a long letter in an email explaining my position and trying to warn this pastor/apostle. It did not go well. I wrote my heart out, and it was met with a simple statement of acceptance and that his doors would always be open to me. I was stunned. That's all he had to say to me? I made some very serious statements and it completely fell on deaf ears, but at least the pastor/apostle could never say he wasn't warned.

There was nothing left to do but leave it all in God's hands. This was one of the darkest moments in my life, and I was devastated. I had to fight not to return to that church. I desperately wanted to feel comfort and believe the lies of the devil. Maybe I was feeling bad because God was punishing me. However, in those moments of despair, God was giving me a choice to make: Would I rely on my feelings, or His word? This was a test, and God was seeing what my faith was built on.

Even though I was tormented inside and couldn't feel God's presence, would I still seek Him, and search His word alone for truth? I asked God for truth, even if it destroyed me, and that was happening. God was helping me come to the full truth and would help me eventually re-write my story. Not only did I experience kundalini in the New Age, but I was being made aware of the false spirits that have entered the churches.

This whole experience really made me question things and learn very quickly to only rely on God's word. It became critical to study it and hide it in my heart. This made me seek God further. I prayed for months, trying to make sense out of all I experienced. Was it all a lie? I mean, my whole life had changed. I did a complete 180. I loved the Lord. I questioned my salvation. What about that intense fire, blissful experience? Was that real? I needed to know if I could trust my own experiences. It's like I needed these experiences to validate God for me. Finally, the answer came from God, and I got chills as I came to this verse.

(1 Kings 19:11-13) Then He said, "Go out, and stand on the mountain before the Lord.*" And behold, the* Lord *passed by, and a great and strong wind tore into the mountains and broke the rocks in pieces before the* Lord, *but the* Lord *was not in the wind; and after the wind an earthquake, but the* Lord *was not in the earthquake; and after the earthquake a fire, but the* Lord *was not in the fire; and after the fire a still small voice. So it was, when Elijah heard it, that he wrapped his face in his mantle and went out and stood in the entrance of the cave...*

Reading these verses struck my heart and spoke to my spirit. All the manifestations, and even the fire experience, were loud noises to get my focus off what mattered. But the evidence of the true Holy Spirit was the quiet voice that lived within me. He was there with me every step of the way, tugging at my heart, showing me the way. Would I hear Him, though? Or would the one who sought to devour roar louder?

In the end, I chose to place God's word above my feelings and understanding. I chose to trust Him when a war waged around me. Most importantly, I chose *truth!* I endured, and I waited for His leading. Jesus truly did heal me; that wasn't fake. The Holy Spirit was really with me, and His presence was everything the Word said He would be: self-control; peace; comfort; love; and, *more than anything, He was truth!*

* * *

God has shown me the narrow path to life, and I am forever grateful for His grace and mercy. I never could have imagined how narrow this path of following Jesus was. I consider it an absolute miracle that I was saved from such an intricate web of lies.

We are living in perilous times that the Bible talked about. It is so important we know who Jesus is through God's word. There is a false gospel and a different Jesus. The Jesus I found in the New Age religion is the same Jesus that exists in the NAR movement. It is a mystical, miracle movement that seeks to bring back office of apostle and prophet who receive new revelation. In this belief system, God's word has merely become a side dish instead of the main course.

The NAR is rapidly growing and will deceive many. The following chapters will go into detail about what this movement is and seek to defend true Biblical doctrine.

CHAPTER 11
SIGNS AND WONDERS

"There is nothing new in theology except that which is false."
(C.H. Spurgeon.)

There is a paradigm shift happening within our culture, resulting in a change of our collective consciousness. Paganism and the occult have infiltrated every facet of society and has insidiously altered Christianity. Syncretism (the amalgamation or attempted amalgamation of different religions, cultures, or schools of thought) is well at work.

Coming out of the New Age made what I experienced in the church seem all too familiar. Many different streams are converging as one. The three streams of the New Apostolic Reformation are the Toronto Blessing, Kansas City prophets, and Bethel Church of Redding California.

It has been said the Spirit of God is doing a "new thing," but the Bible has already said, *There is nothing new under the sun.* ***(Ecclesiastes 1:9.)***

In this chapter, we will explain what the New Apostolic Reformation is and how we got this far. We have placed emphasis on supernatural phenomenon, experiences, and seeking after a sign. Christianity is moving from a Biblical Gospel of hearing the Word and faith, to a gospel of signs and "encounters."

Jesus is the Word made manifest. It is His word that spoke creation into existence, and it is His word that will finally destroy

115

all evil. We have now replaced Bible studies with supernatural schools of ministry. The emphasis is placed on us and our "destinies," instead of the will of God.

Christians are being groomed to accept a form of new spirituality and being disarmed of the only weapon they have… *The Bible.* I'm afraid false spirits have entered the church, and many people are seeking gifts instead of the gift-giver. Professing Christians now attend conferences to soak up the next great anointing and seek to get "high" and "drunk in the Spirit." People are having "Holy Ghost Parties," and "the Spirit" is making them laugh uncontrollably. Inhibitions have been lowered, and nobody is alert and vigilant.

(1 Peter 5:8) *Be sober, be vigilant; because your adversary the devil walks about like a roaring lion, seeking whom he may devour.*

This warning has fallen on deaf ears, while God's people remain spiritually intoxicated. The New Apostolic Reformation believes God is restoring apostles and prophets to the church. It is also a signs-and-wonders movement. Much of the supernatural manifestations seen in churches began with the Toronto Blessing revival.

The Toronto Blessing phenomenon happened in Toronto, Canada, in 1994. It started with a group of 100 people, who all experienced phenomena such as falling to the floor, laughter, crying, convulsing, and some even roaring like animals. Within a year, it grew to 1,000 people. People would fly in from all around the world and from many different denominations.

The phenomenon was so extravagant that it garnered attention from magazines and news sources interested in this new outpouring of "the Spirit." Many were tired of cold, dead religion and asked God for something more. Sometimes God will give us exactly what we are asking for.

An article entitled, "Laughing for the Lord," was featured in TIME Magazine, and, during a taped episode of CBC's "Sunday Morning" in Canada, a reporter can be heard debriefing the revival.

"A young woman is lying on the floor with her eyes closed. As she speaks, her body jerks ever so slightly. All around her people are laughing or crying or shaking uncontrollably... (in the background is maniacal shrill laughter)... This is what the Vineyard Church calls the Holy Spirit's joy of laughter. They aren't laughing at anything being said, they are just laughing." (Weighed and Found Wanting: The Toronto Experience Examined in the Light of the Bible, Bill Randles, Page 13.)

Many at this revival are believing this is what was prophesied in **Joel 2:28**: *And it shall come to pass afterward that I will pour out My Spirit on all flesh.* They are believing this is a second Pentecost, and many give little heed to Biblical warnings of deception in the last days: a deception so grand that, if possible, even God's very elect would be deceived.

(Mathew 24:24) *For false christs and false prophets will rise and show great signs and wonders to deceive, if possible, even the elect.*

Instead, this new, emergent movement would give birth to experiential faith rather than Biblical faith. Watching a video of the Toronto Blessing, instead of Jesus as the focus, there are countless people moved by extreme emotional experiences, and many testify about themselves and how their lives are radically changed.

It is mentioned, in John, chapter 15, that when the Holy Spirit comes, He will not testify of Himself but always point one to Jesus.

(John 15:26) *But when the Helper comes, whom I shall send to you from the Father, the Spirit of truth who proceeds from the Father, He will testify of Me.*

These meetings erupt in chaos and disorderly conduct which is against God's nature. God is a God of order, and nothing is more important than the preaching of His word. However, many times at churches like the Toronto Blessing, there is no preaching of the Word because it is often interrupted by uncontrollable laughing.

During interviews of the Toronto Blessing, it is touted that participants are from many different cultures, races, and denominations, as well as different socioeconomic statuses. There are physicians, supreme court judges, socialists, and ministers, ranging from Catholic to Baptist. It is reported that marriages are being healed and many experience profound feelings of love and unity. Many will even break out in spontaneous laughter while on camera.

What's interesting about this new outpouring is not only the push for unification between congregants but the similar phenomenology as many other cults. The strange manifestations are found nowhere in the Bible, yet are seen in kundalini cults, qigong movements, Sufism, and even Franz Mezmer's healing occult practice.

Many proponents of this Toronto movement believe that these manifestations resemble popular revivals of old, such as those led by John Wesley and Charles Finney. However, it is well known to many who studied past revivals that bizarre manifestations usually began flooding in towards the end of revival, when the devil was trying to destroy or discredit it. In the Bible we are warned to "test the spirits" because not every supernatural occurrence is from God.

In a book written by T.W. Caskey, about revivals in the 1800s, it is said, *"Some would fall prostrate and lie helpless for hours at a time... The whole congregation, by some inexplicable nervous action, would sometimes be thrown into side-splitting convulsions of laughter and when it started, no power could check or control it until it ran its course. When a man started laughing, dancing, shouting, and jerking, it was impossible to stop until, exhausted, nature broke down into a death-like swoon..."*

The same writer began to wonder if these manifestations were from the Holy Spirit, and people began to test the spirits more, often ending the bizarre manifestations. True revival always seemed to be marked by deep sorrow and conviction of sin, and people like John Wesley were often suspicious of strange phenomenon.

John Wesley came across many demonic manifestations and writes about them in his journals. On one occasion, John Wesley describes, *"God suffered Satan to teach them better. Both were suddenly seized in the manner as the rest and laughed whether they would, or no, almost without ceasing. This they continued for two days, a spectacle to all, and were then, upon prayer, delivered in a moment." (Toronto Controversy–Disturbing New Facts from History.)*

If these manifestations died out because of testing the spirits back then, perhaps we are failing that same test now and opening the doors to a wide-open welcome to foreign spirits that exist to deceive.

Many that attended this revival would get an impartation and then bring back this spirit to their own churches. This was the beginning of a paradigm shift and change over to experiential or mystical, Christianity. Prior to the Toronto Blessing, Pastors Bill and Carol Arnott were inspired by a revival in Argentina that was like the Toronto outpouring.

Much of the Toronto Blessing can be attributed to a man named Rodney Howard Brown, who calls himself the "Holy Ghost bartender." He is a pastor/apostle from South Africa, who, according to his own testimony, experienced holy laughter after being in desperation for a touch from God. He yelled at God, "If you don't come down here right now and touch me, I'm going to die and come up there and touch you!"

After commanding God, he suddenly started to feel a fire strike through his whole body, and a bubbling out of his stomach of "living water." He started to laugh uncontrollably and become drunk on "the Spirit." This lasted for several days afterwards.

In 1989, during a series of meetings in New York, Brown began to see several people fall out of their seats. It would look like people were shooting at them and whole rows of people would go down. Many were laughing and weeping. Many at this meeting would go on to pioneer the Toronto Blessing.

Rodney Howard Brown, on TBN channel, said that "holy laughter" was a last-days expression of God's Holy Spirit. There were also many prophecies prior to Toronto, speaking of a new-signs-and-wonders movement. In July of 1993, while visiting Vancouver, Marc Dupont shared a vision of a new power coming to the Toronto churches.

"There will be two stages. The first will be related to Ezekiel's vision of dry bones receiving flesh. The second stage will include powerful signs and wonders... It will be trans-denominational but will be conditional on prior operation of the full five-fold ministry specified in Ephesians 4:11." (A Chronicle of the Toronto Blessing and Other Related Events, David Hilborn, Page 15.)

It's interesting to note that presently the New Apostolic Reformation often refers to itself as a five-fold ministry and seeks to be inter-denominational.

One of the key players of the New Apostolic Reformation and Mystical Miracle Movement is Bill Johnson, from Bethel Church of Redding California. Bill Johnson attended the Toronto Blessing before becoming the lead pastor/apostle of Bethel Church.

Toronto, Bethel Church, and Kansas City Prophets are known as the "three rivers" that have been prophesied to become one stream from three rivers. In 2011, during a "Three-stream conference," in Toronto, Bill and Beni Johnson and the Arnott's were discussing the convergence prophecy.

"The converging of these three streams will bring fuller revelation of the Trinity to the Body of Christ, help us usher in the great end-time revival and raise the water level to an extent we can only attain together. We are seeing the fulfilment of prophecy." (NAR Prophets Claim the Three Streams will be One, Amy Spreeman, BereanResearch.org.)

The Toronto Blessing was a pivotal event that helped birth the Signs & Wonders Movement. This "stream" awakened people's consciousness to a new form of spirituality, one of supernatural power and an answer to what many were seeking. As floods of people attended this event, they would subsequently get "imparted" with this spirit and bring it back to their own churches.

Was this part of a great end-times revival or the opening of a great end-times deception? I cannot find one scripture that points to an end-times prophecy predicting a "great revival." In II Thessalonians 2, it speaks of a great apostasy.

(2 Thessalonians 2:3-11) Let no one deceive you by any means; for that day will not come unless the falling away comes first, and

the man of sin is revealed, the son of perdition, who opposes and exalts himself above all that is called God or that is worshiped, so that he sits as God in the temple of God, showing himself that he is God. Do you not remember that when I was still with you, I told you these things? And now you know what is restraining, that he may be revealed in his own time. For the mystery of lawlessness is already at work; only He who now restrains will do so until He is taken out of the way. And then the lawless one will be revealed, whom the Lord will consume with the breath of His mouth and destroy with the brightness of His coming. The coming of the lawless one is according to the working of Satan, with all power, signs, and lying wonders, and with all unrighteous deception among those who perish, because they did not receive the love of the truth, that they might be saved. And for this reason, God will send them strong delusion, that they should believe the lie.

This is not a warning to take lightly. Most people will willingly accept anything as "God" and do not take any Biblical warnings seriously. If there is going to be an end-times deception, shouldn't we tread more carefully? We know that even God's elect could be deceived and that Satan is coming with all-powerful signs and wonders, and he will sit in the temple pretending to be God, and many will perish because they love not truth (God's word). (*2 Thessalonians 2:10.*)

Shouldn't we be defending ourselves with the scripture? Shouldn't we be searching it night and day to make sure we are not deceived?

If we look closely at Toronto, we will see the tapestry of unity woven in. The manifestations that occurred match perfectly to those of the occult; and, like the occult, there is an underlying motive to intertwine faith. The occult is not afraid to mention Jesus' name—as long as it is a different Jesus, the mystical one outside the confines of scripture. What a perfect way to unify.

The Toronto Blessing is mystical Christianity and unleashes a spirit that intoxicates, seducing Christians to judge with their hearts instead of their minds. In an article written in the *Evangelical Studies Bulletin* called, "*The Spirit and the Bride: The*

Toronto Blessing and Church Structure," it speaks of a unifying perspective.

"The 'Toronto Blessing' in North America remains, at this point in time, a subculture within a subculture. The Toronto Blessing has the potential to not only revitalize a faltering p/c movement but to break out of evangelical subculture. It offers a fresh presentation of the basic gospel message that could serve as a Christian voice to postmodernists and provide a Christian alternative for the popular New Age movement... As a newly emergent religious movement that has touched believers and churches on all continents, the Toronto Blessing has the potential to offer the Western world an alternative Christian perspective that is truly catholic." (The Spirit and the Bride: The Toronto Blessing and the Church Structure, Margaret Poloma, Paragraph 19, hirr.hartsem.edu.)

The Toronto Blessing was a pivotal point in Christianity and how we do church. A true revival brings repentance, holiness, and purity, as well as evangelism. False revivals bring fleshly manifestations, counterfeit signs/giftings, and casting off our inhibitions. It allows us to forget testing of spirits and reverence for Holy Scriptures.

In our glory of drunken stupor, we have allowed Satan to feast upon our will and emotions and join a cult of unity, based on experience and *love*. As we look at the three streams of NAR, we see it as Toronto, Bethel Church, and Kansas City Prophets. These three movements are essentially changing the face of Christianity. The New Apostolic Reformation is exactly that: a reform as big as the original reformation from Catholicism, only now that change is leading us back to Rome and mysticism. It is abolishing salvation by grace, through faith in Christ alone.

Seeking excesses in the Signs & Wonders Movement reflects one of little faith. It is adding to the Word of God by seeking a salvation other than Christ alone. We are moving away from sola scriptura and replacing it with Christian mysticism.

Christian mysticism is having a direct experience with God and, therefore, bypassing doctrine. It is considered an inner knowing which is subjective truth.

This is the same thing we see in New Age beliefs, where truth is subjective instead of concrete. Mysticism is very much esoteric and leads to hidden knowledge or *gnosis*. This is exactly what Gnosticism is, and it is taking over Biblical Christianity.

The New Apostolic Reformation is a movement that not only believes in restoring the office of apostle and prophet but also one that is allowing a trojan horse of mysticism to infiltrate on a global scale. This new reformation is changing the face of Christianity and is dismantling its very foundation by building upon it with the continuation of apostles and prophets, many of whom consider themselves equal or better than the original twelve. These power positions within the church hold special authority and "anointings," often brainwashing their followers to have unquestioning devotion. The new emphasis is on feelings, experiences, destinies, and the elevation of man. Even in my own church, services revolved around conjuring up the presence of the "Holy Spirit." People have begun to develop an insatiable desire to encounter some divine presence. Scripture is no longer enough, and now we demand something more.

Much of what is being experienced is in direct contradiction to the Bible but with Christian-sounding lingo to cover up its occult origins. Instead of us heeding the warning to remain vigilant and sober minded, we have become "drunk in the Spirit." Instead of reverence that produces fear of the Lord, we now mock with "Holy laughter." And we have now traded Bible studies for supernatural schools of ministry, where we can pay to learn and earn the gifts of God.

Most importantly, we have failed to *"be ye separate from the world," (2 Corinthians 6:17)*. Instead, we've "redeemed" the occult, and told ourselves we can make it our own. This is evident in books such as, *The Physics of Heaven*, by Bill Johnson, which we will discuss later. The New Apostolic beliefs are hard to pin down, as many do not affiliate with this title. It is a broad movement, evangelizing many with a seductive and sensual gospel, appealing to man's flesh.

Many in the NAR camp will deny its existence and say that it is a title made up by those opposing the spiritual gifts. Instead, those within NAR will identify themselves with titles such as, "the five-fold ministry," or "the prophetic movement." However, those that insist the NAR doesn't exist haven't done their homework. "The New Apostolic Reformation" was a title coined by its own founder, C. Peter Wagner.

C. Peter Wagner was planning a seminary course on this movement and needed to come up with a name. This movement was meant to reach between interdenominational lines and bring it under the guise of unity. As he was coming up with a name, first it was going to be "Independent Charismatic," but he decided that not all churches are charismatic.

According to Wagner, *"The name I have settled on is the New Apostolic Reformation. I use "reformation" because, as I have said, these new wineskins appear to be at least as radical as those of the protestant reformation almost 500 years ago."* (Transforming Power of Revival, Chapter 14.)

So, as we can see, this is a real name, given by its founder, with intentions to reform the face of Christianity as we know it. C. Peter Wagner gave his own explanation for what this New Apostolic Reformation entails. In a book called, "*The Transforming Power of Revival: prophetic Strategies into the 21*st *Century,"* Wagner outlines, in chapter 14, his church growth experiences and his paradigm shift into the Signs & Wonders Movement, which ultimately led to his forming of the New Apostolic Reformation.

We will look at the several *new* ways the structure of church has been set up to change in the NAR.

- **There is a new authority structure:** *"The amount of spiritual authority delegated by the Holy Spirit to individuals. Pastors are merely employees. But the NAR apostles are leaders of the church."* (Transforming Power of Revival, Chapter 14.)

- **There is new leadership training:** The focus is helping people walk in their gifts. However, what has become scary is the fact that Bible school is now considered "remote."

"Continuing education for leadership takes place in conferences, seminars, and retreats, rather than accredited institutions." (Transforming Power of Revival, Chapter 14.)

The focus of education is being taken away from the Bible and is taking on a new theology of displaying powerful gifts of "the Spirit." It is a system of elitism.

Something seen at many of these NAR conferences is receiving "impartations" of a spirit and then taking it back to other churches. It is spreading like a virus.

- **There is new ministry focus:** "New Apostolic ministries are vision driven." (*The Transforming Power of revival, C. Peter Wagner, Chapter 14.*)

  The question I beg is, *who's vision?* Usually New Apostolic pastors/apostles are talking about the vision that stems from whatever church leadership believes the Holy Spirit has specially revealed to them. These so-called visions for ministry are not rooted in scripture.

- **There is a new worship style:** *"Worship leaders have replaced music directors, keyboards have replaced organs, casual worship teams have replaced robed choirs. Ten to twelve minutes of singing is now forty-nine minutes or more." (The Transforming Power of Revival, C. peter Wagner, Chapter 14.)*

  As I can attest from my own experience, worship could turn into an hour or more session, singing repetitive chants to usher in a "presence" and induce a hypnotic experience.

- **There are new prayer forms:** *"Prayer in New Apostolic churches has taken forms rarely seen in traditional* *congregations. Some of this takes place within the church, and some takes place outside the church." (Transforming Power of Revival, C. Peter Wagner, Chapter 14.)*

- **There is new financing:** "Generous giving is expected. Tithing is without apology, and those who do not tithe their incomes are subtly encouraged to evaluate their Christian lives as subpar." (Transforming Power of Revival, C. Peter Wagner, Chapter 14.)

- **There are new outreaches:** *"Aggressively reaching out to the lost and hurting of the community, the world, is part of the New Apostolic DNA." (Transforming Power of Revival, C. Peter Wagner, Chapter 14.)*

  You will notice in these movements there is a lot of talk on changing one's DNA through the activation of the Holy Spirit. This is also spoken of in the New Age movement as a type of evolving spiritual man.

- **There is new power orientation:** NAR churches believe in supernatural power; they believe all gifts are active for today and view the book of Acts as prescriptive instead of descriptive.

  "It is commonplace to observe active ministries of healing, demonic deliverance, spiritual warfare, prophecy, falling in the Spirit, spiritual mapping, prophetic acts, fervent intercession and so on. More emphasis on the heart than on the mind." (Transforming Power of Revival, C. Peter Wagner, Chapter 14.)

C. Peter Wagner had an agenda which is outlined: Its success is viewed by Wagner as "unity+spiritual gifts=growth." Now, unity is important for God's true church, but the NAR is unifying over spiritual experiences instead of doctrine, which is to deny true "fruit of the Spirit."

(Galatians 5:22-23) But the fruit of the Spirit is love, joy, peace, longsuffering, kindness, goodness, faithfulness, gentleness, self-control. Against such there is no law.

The Bible tells us in the Book of Matthew, *"We will know them by their fruits." (Matthew 7:20.)*

And Jesus Himself tells us, *"I did not come to bring peace but a sword." (Matthew 10:34.)*

This is because truth will never unify, but, instead, it separates those that desire to hear it from those that don't.

The New Apostolic Reformation is the fastest growing form of Christianity on a global level but has crept into most churches unaware. It has infiltrated largely by way of popular worship music (such as Bethel music and Jesus Culture.) It has advertised itself as a fresh, new way of doing church. Often those proclaim, "No more boring church!"

In my own church, a prophet announced to our congregation, "God will no longer put up with religious spirits!"

If people do not conform to this *new* move of God, they will be missing out on this great world revival. Statements like these are what prevent any questioning of the Apostolic leadership.

After I left the prophetic church, I was alarmed at the many programs in churches that stem from popular Bethel Church of Redding California. In my small state of Connecticut, I found many similar schools of supernatural ministry. In Redding, California, Bethel Church has a large school called BSSM (Bethel School of Supernatural Ministry). It is here that a younger generation learns about the "Gospel of the Kingdom" and acquiring spiritual gifts. Students fly in from all around the globe.

If you look through their curriculum, most of the required reading is by the leaders of Bethel and very little Bible. Places like these are becoming indoctrination centers for the younger generation. We have now made the Bible about us instead of about Jesus.

Those in the NAR movement believe we are living in a time of a second Pentecost. The NAR is nothing new but can trace its roots back to the "Latter Rain" movement." The Latter Rain movement, in the 1940's, taught that God was pouring out a "latter rain," before our Lord returns, just like the days of Pentecost. This movement was centered around revival meetings that took place in Saskatchewan, Canada. This movement, like the NAR, believes in the divine and the restoration of apostles and prophets. The Assemblies of God churches denounced this movement in 1949.

When the Latter Rain began, it was called, "The last great outpouring that was to consummate God's plans on this earth." A book called the *"Atomic Power with God,"* by Franklin Hall, influenced many involved in the Latter Rain.

Franklin Hall taught on revival doctrine centered on fasting and subduing the earth as well as a "body-felt salvation." Franklin Hall promoted a baptism where one could be free from sin and sickness, called the "Holy Ghost fire."

In this body-felt salvation, he claimed that it was "700% greater than ordinary healing power." His teachings taught that this great baptism would "heal from all sickness, tiredness, and even body odor." It also promised that one could achieve immortality.

In the previous chapter, I told my story of undergoing a profound supernatural experience that felt like fire burning through my body and spirit. It felt like, a "body-felt" salvation, and, in many ways, it made me feel elite. I felt special and my salvation hung on this experience, as if God had specially anointed me and gave me the experience I craved.

The New Apostolic Reformation differs from the Latter Rain only by title, but its doctrines are the same. The Latter Rain movement was steeped in elitism, and it was believed this outpouring would be even greater than that of the Book of Acts.

A man named Bill Hamon became involved with Wagner and brought the Latter Rain doctrine into the New Apostolic Reformation from its very beginning. C. Peter Wagner wrote the foreword to Bill Hamon's book, *"Apostles, Prophets and the Coming Moves of God: God's End-Time Plans for His Church and Planet earth."*

Bill Hamon taught on the Manifest Sons of God doctrine. According to Hamon, *"The Manifest sons of God doctrine teaches that these sons will be equal to Jesus Christ: immortal, sinless, perfected sons who have partaken of the divine nature. They have every right to be called gods and will be gods." (The Manifest Sons of God of the Latter Rain Movement, Paragraph 19, letusreason.org, 2016.)*

Bill Hamon taught that the sons of God will be subduing the earth for Christ to reappear. *"Widespread spiritual warfare will result with the sons of God doing battle with Satan, the non-Christian nations of this world will be defeated. Once the earth is subdued, Jesus will come back to earth." (The Generations of Antichrist: An Argument for the Sake of Heaven, G.H. Eliason, Page 33.)*

Bill Hamon rejects the rapture, and the Manifest Sons of God doctrine is the birthing place for Kingdom Now or Dominion theology. Dominionism is a big part of what the NAR teaches, and we will discuss this further.

C. Peter Wagner was very much a visionary on how the church structure would change. Those in the church are rising to leadership, not by training at an accredited institution but by being trained in conferences, by receiving an "anointing." Instead of "studying to show thyself approved *(2 Timothy 2:15)*," we can now grab and get whatever gift we choose by having someone "impart" them to us.

This rise of mystical Christianity has fooled us into having an insatiable desire to feed our flesh with our carnal desires. Like a drug addict, followers of NAR attend conference after conference, searching for their next high. We need to see, hear, feel, smell, and taste God. He must appeal to or our sensuality. Many Christians in this movement think they are becoming more spiritual, when, instead, they are only becoming more carnal.

(2 Peter 2:2) And many will follow their destructive ways, because of whom the way of truth will be blasphemed.

The warning in second Peter is exactly what is happening. We have placed experience above truth. The authority structure is changing. Instead of an organization or governing church body, we sometimes have a single apostle as overseer of the church with zero accountability for anything, including finances. Because of their title and hierarchy, they are seldom questioned, and many will follow them with a cult-like intensity.

Apostles and prophets have risen in the church to a guru-like status. This is very common in Christian cults: There is usually a hierarchy and those who are carrying special authority over the people. Like in cults, those underneath leadership are forbidden to question. It's interesting to note some of the common traits. Let's take a brief look at these.

- *"The group displays excessively zealous and unquestioning commitment to its leader." (Characteristics of Cults, Janja Lalich, and Michael Langone, Paragraph 4, apologeticsindex.org.)*

  Often those who question beliefs are referred to as having religious spirits, Jezebel spirits, or they are accused of not being led by the Holy Spirit.

- *"Questioning, doubt, and dissent are discouraged or even punished." (Characteristics of Cults, Janja Lalich, and Michael Langone, Paragraph 4, apologeticsindex.org.)*

- *"Mind-altering practices, such as meditation, chanting, speaking in tongues, denunciation sessions, and debilitating work routines are used in excess." (Characteristics of Cults, Janja Lalich, and Michael Langone, Paragraph 4, apologeticsindex.org.)*

  Those in the NAR camps put themselves into a hypnotic, trance state, listening to repetitive, seductive worship music. Speaking in ecstatic tongues can induce a hypnotic state as well, and many are encouraged to chant in tongues, denying scripture which commands all things to be done decently and in order.

- *"The group is elitist, claiming a special, exalted status for itself, its leaders, and members." (Characteristics of Cults,*

Janja Lalich, and Michael Langone, Paragraph 4, apologeticsindex.org.)

In NAR, apostles and prophets hold special status, and those not part of this "new move of God" are not anointed. In other words, they are lacking in the Holy Spirit.

- *"The group has a polarized, us-versus-them mentality, which may cause conflict with wider society." (Characteristics of Cults, Janja Lalich, and Michael Langone, Paragraph 4, apologeticsindex.org.)*

Those in NAR believe in Kingdom Now, with a take-over-the-world mentality. Those who do not conform, either inside or outside the church, are going to be enemies. This new breed of sanctified Christians, has the authority to judge and cleanse the earth.

- "The leadership induces feelings of shame and/or guilt in order to influence and/or control." (*Characteristics of Cults, Janja Lalich, and Michael Langone, Paragraph 4, apologeticsindex.org.)*

- *"The group is preoccupied with making money and bringing in new members." (Characteristics of Cults, Janja Lalich, and Michael Langone, Paragraph 4, apologeticsindex.org.)*

In NAR camps, tithing is often pressured, and blessings are promised to those who significantly tithe. Also, they hold conferences and events, trying to reach vast numbers of people. It is about numbers, not discipleship.

- "Members are encouraged or required to live and/or socialize only with other group members." (*Characteristics of Cults, Janja Lalich, and Michael Langone, Paragraph 4, apologeticsindex.org.)*

In popular churches, such as Bethel Church, there have been testimonies of children attending BSSM and cutting off their family members. Through methods such as SOZO, inner healing participants remember false memories of abuse, and families are destroyed.

* * *

Ministry focus is shifting. It's no longer about the Gospel of Jesus Christ but about the "gospel of the kingdom." It is about bringing heaven to earth, with less regard for eternity. NAR churches are constantly seeking "revival," signs, wonders, and chasing the "presence" of God. Biblical Christianity is about faith, not chasing signs and manifestations.

(Matthew 16:4) A wicked and adulterous generation seeks after a sign...

The "gospel of the kingdom" is related to Kingdom Now theology, and participants believe we are setting up God's kingdom here on earth. A new worship style has emerged, with tunes that are breathtaking, albeit seductive, and enchanting. The music romanticizes our relationship to Jesus, and the lyrics are often theologically wrong.

Popular music such as, Bethel, Jesus Culture, and Hillsong have become favorites to play at many churches. While many churches have welcomed this new worship style, it has also opened its doors to their church programs and doctrines. We now worship to "shift atmospheres," and "open heavenly portals." Why the constant seeking of a presence? Does the Holy Spirit not live within us? Psalm 139 teaches us that we can't go anywhere that God is not with us.

(Psalm 139:7-10) Where can I go from Your Spirit? Or where can I flee from Your presence? If I ascend into heaven, You are there; if I make my bed in hell, behold, You are there. If I take the wings of the morning, and dwell in the uttermost parts of the sea, even there Your hand shall lead me, and Your right hand shall hold me.

New prayer forms have taken over, but Jesus taught us how we should pray: *"And when you pray, do not use vain repetitions*

as the heathen do. For they think that they will be heard for their
many words. Therefore, do not be like them. For your Father knows
the things you have need of before you ask Him. In this manner,
therefore, pray:

> *Our Father in heaven,*
> *Hallowed be Your name.*
> *Your kingdom come.*
> *Your will be done*
> *On earth as it is in heaven.*
> *Give us this day our daily bread.*
> *And forgive us our debts,*
> *As we forgive our debtors.*
> *And do not lead us into temptation,*
> *But deliver us from the evil one.*
> *For Yours is the kingdom and the power and the glory for-*
> *ever. Amen.*
> **(Matthew 6:7-13.)**

Now, our focus on prayer has come straight out of New Age
practices. We no longer pray for God's will to be done but instead
impose our own will and treat the Almighty as a personal genie.

While reading a quote on Bill Johnson's website, I came
across, *"Don't pray as God's will be done; prayers never get answered*
that way."

That is appalling and contradicting what Jesus taught. In
churches, the focus is now on contemplative prayer, "soaking"
prayer (which is akin to transcendental meditation), circle prayers,
and even labyrinth-type prayers. These all have more in common
with witchcraft than they do with Biblical Christianity.

Then we have a new outreach coupled with a "new-power
orientation." The church is reaching beyond its church doors,
which is good, but the true gospel isn't being preached. Instead,
the focus is on an "encounter" and healing demonstrations that
liken the Holy Spirit to some sort of magic trick.

The Bible says that "faith comes by hearing," not by showing. The Word says that signs/wonders would *follow* the gospel, not *lead*. There are many conferences, such as The Awakening, in Australia, which attracts droves of people to experience God through manifestations and get saved through some sort of power encounter. The title alone sounds New Age. What exactly are we awakening?

The NAR has seen explosive growth and has taken over in places like Africa, South America, Asia, and Australia. Are we truly making disciples, or mass false converts? NAR also places emphasis on strategic spiritual warfare, where NAR apostles can take over territories and regions where demonic principalities lie. This, again, is putting man in a powerful position that can cause more harm than good. Not even the archangel, Michael, would dare rebuke the devil.

(Jude 1:9) Yet Michael the archangel, in contending with the devil, when he disputed about the body of Moses, dared not bring against him a reviling accusation, but said, "The Lord rebuke you!"

God never commands us to fight the devil head on. We are not God, and our victory comes through our submission to Christ. Chasing the devil out of territories, deliverance ministries, and inner-healing ministries, such as SOZO, are adding to Christ's finished work on the cross.

(John 8:36) Therefore, if the Son makes you free, you shall be free indeed.

Deliverance and inner healing ministries promise to set people free, while leading the unsuspecting into bondage. SOZO, for example, is an inner-healing ministry that originated in Bethel Redding. It puts people into a hypnotic state, while recovering past (false) memories that have torn families apart. This type of inner healing doesn't abide by Christian principles and has its roots in theosophy.

The definition of theosophy is, "Any of a number of philosophies maintaining that a knowledge of God may be achieved through spiritual ecstasy, direct intuition, or special individual relations, especially the movement founded in 1875 as the

Theosophical Society, by Helena Blavatsky and Henry Steel Olcott (1832–1907.)"

SOZO means "saved, healed and delivered," in Greek. This method was created by Dawna Desilva after attending Bethel Church in 1997. According to the Bethel SOZO team, *"Inner healing and deliverance ministry is aimed to get to the root of things hindering your personal connection with the Father, Son, and Holy Spirit. With a healed connection, you can walk in the destiny to which you have been called." (What is Sozo? Paragraph 1, bethelsozo.com.)*

With their special tools, they can give you something extra that the Bible never talks about. If your connection to the Trinity is compromised, you might want to look at sin. Sin and lack of obedience is what separates us from God, (**Isaiah 59:2**).

SOZO uses tools such as Father Ladder, The Four Doors, Presenting Jesus, and the Wall. Being put into a suggestible state to meet "Jesus" and help Him bring you back to your childhood memories is opening doors to your life to encounter false spirits.

(Philippians 3:13-14) *Brethren, I do not count myself to have apprehended; but one thing I do, forgetting those things which are behind and reaching forward to those things which are ahead, I press toward the goal for the prize of the upward call of God in Christ Jesus.*

Jesus is not interested in looking at your past or trauma. He has made you a new creation, and your identity is wrapped in Him.

Orrel Steinkamp says it best with regards to inner healing: *"Christianized inner healing internally regresses a person into his/her past and, by various mystical and outright shamanistic procedures, then introduces the "actual, real, living" Jesus within the person's altered state of consciousness. By this procedure, the past mystically becomes present. The conjured Jesus figure will not only heal the past but will change the facts of history in order to bring about the desired healing." (Divinization Finds Further Expression in the Evangelical Church, The Plumbline, Volume 9, 2004, Paragraph 16, 4truthministry.com.)*

These methods are not Biblical and are taking Christians captive to deceit. The New Apostolic Reformation is changing the face of Christianity, and the way of truth is being blasphemed. As New-Age practices are infiltrating, Biblical understanding is becoming less important.

A very important doctrine that has taken over is "Dominion" or "Kingdom Now" theology. The end-times church is not looking up for our blessed Savior but instead "Christianizing" the land, taking over the "seven spheres of influence." This is known as the Seven Mountain Mandate. The seven mountains include education, religion, family, business, government/military, arts/entertainment, and media.

You will often hear those in NAR camps say things such as, "The Kingdom of heaven suffers violence, and the violent take it by force." This is a verse taken out of context from Matthew 11:12. Jesus and the disciples never commanded world takeover; He commanded to simply make disciples and spread the true gospel.

The NAR cult, mixed with Kingdom Now theology is taking over churches, disregarding scripture, syncretizing with the New Age, and preparing to take over the kingdoms of the world. What about those Christians who won't conform? What about those unwilling to accept these "new wineskins," choosing to believe scripture over manmade doctrine? Well, they will need to be removed and the earth cleansed of them. According to NAR beliefs, Jesus won't return until His Kingdom has been set up—by mere man—here on earth. It is Kingdom Now adherents who must usher in Christ's return.

"A seductive shift has occurred where leaders and teachers falsely believe their ministries and churches are the manifestation of the Kingdom of Heaven on earth. As a result, "little kingdoms," and "little gods" run the world for God in His place… Worldly success has blinded them from realizing many things valued in the eyes of man can be a reproach to God." (Kingdom Come: A Biblical Response to Dominion Theology, Don Pirozok, Page. 110.)

We have New-Age practices entering the church, coupled with Biblical illiteracy and cleansing the earth of those who get in the way, all while welcoming the return of "Christ." This is very close to occult/New Age doctrine, which seeks to also evolve humanity to become co-redeemers of the earth—and those who do not evolve will need to disappear. We will discuss this more in depth in the coming chapter.

Dominion Theology is intertwined with Manifest Sons of God doctrine. This teaches that in the last days a super breed of Christians will have supernatural power and be instrumental in subduing the earth. It is believed that the "manifest sons of God" will be perfected into glorified bodies prior to Christ's return.

Many in the NAR camp believe in a Kingdom Now agenda known as, "Joel's Army." Joel's army sees itself as an end-times army that will perform miracles, take dominion of the earth, and execute judgement. Rick Joyner, from Morningstar Ministries, speaks of a coming civil war between Christians.

Joyner states, *"What is about to come to earth is not just revival, or another awakening; it is verifiable revolution. This vision was given in order to begin awakening those who are destined to radically change the course and even the very definition of Christianity." (The Harvest, Rick Joyner, under book description quote by author.)*

Rick Joyner speaks of destroying those passive Christians who refuse to unite with them. The New order of Dominionists will take over.

Manifest Sons of God is pushing the boundaries of the supernatural, teaching we can become as gods. Christians are looking to Jesus as their model for what they can also become. This brings me to another heretical doctrine that fits quite nicely with Dominion theology, and that is kenotic theology. This is taught by many in NAR, with Bill Johnson being a popular teacher of it.

Kenosis teaches that Jesus laid aside His divinity and had to function as an anointed man, relying on the Holy Spirit to give Him His power. *"He teaches the emptying of Christ's divine nature makes the miracles which Jesus Christ performed coming from a man and not His divinity. A faulty conclusion of the source and authority of miracles as well as the nature of Jesus Christ. Pure heresy born out of need for the church to work miracles just like Jesus Christ (a man) in order to transform the nations before the second coming."*

(Kingdom Come: A Biblical Response to Dominion Theology, Don Pirozok, Page 89.)

We now have a whole generation walking around who are subtly denying Jesus' divinity and claiming he had to be born again. This is no different than when Christian cults teach that Jesus was less than God and someone we could emulate (Christ consciousness). At no point did Jesus ever leave behind His divinity. He has always been God and will always be so. If at any point Jesus is less than fully God and fully man, then you have a false Jesus and a different gospel.

As I have said before, New Apostolic Reformation is nothing new. *"There is nothing new under the sun, and nothing that hasn't been done under the sun." (Ecclesiastes 1:9.)*

As Don Pizorak states in his book *"Kingdom Come,"* Page 71, *"This is the age-old temptation, going back into antiquity, working with the mighty men of the earth. Nimrod, the founder of Babylon, is one of the Fathers of religious government rule over the masses of earth. This is an invention of Satan and will result in "Mystery Babylon" joining the kings of the earth to prostitute the church... It is the charismatic church's version of having mini popes who are building kingdoms after their own wills and putting God's label on it."*

Kingdom Now is preparing those to follow the antichrist spirit. This new breed of Christianity does not exist in Holy Scripture and is leading people to complete apostasy. Jesus said His true disciples would keep His word: going throughout the world and making disciples. He never once said we should take over the world and make ourselves into god-men. The Kingdom Now crowd even believes they have the right to call down judgement from heaven. There is only one with that kind of authority, and that is Jesus.

Jesus isn't waiting for man to subdue the earth but has asked us to be ready, as no one knows the day or the hour of His return *(Matthew 24:36)*. He is coming back as judge and is the only one who holds all power and authority.

The doctrine the NAR relies upon is a lie from the ruler of this world. The same lie is offered to Jesus during the 40 days that He was tempted by the devil in the wilderness. This is what Satan said—bear in mind, these are the things the devil possesses and so is allowed to give.

(Matthew 4:8-9) Again, the devil took Him up on an exceedingly high mountain and showed Him all the kingdoms of the world and their glory. And he said to Him, "All these things I will give You if You will fall down and worship me."

Jesus has made it clear that His kingdom is not from this world. It is amazing to me to see the clear scripture being ignored. Satan is whispering to Jesus' followers the same temptation: it is the world he will give you. That price tag, however, is eternal damnation.

Perhaps this "Gospel of the Kingdom" is really a manmade pursuit of the kingdoms of this world that Satan promised. Those who adhere strictly to scripture only are being looked at in a negative light, much the same way the New Age movement views us.

Rick Joyner, from Morningstar Ministries, speaks to his congregation about a civil war that is going to pin Christian against Christian. He believes those involved in this movement are called the "blues," while those who oppose it are called the "grays." Blue stands for revelation, expanse, and openness of spirit, while gray represents logic, the brain. Joyner believes the blues are a "new breed" and are going to build God's Kingdom here on earth.

"Joyner stated that they would be overcome and destroyed in the fight for the true church to evolve to the next level. It may be necessary for us to assist God in finishing up the job. Let me put this in plain English—the Blues were going to help God kill them." (The View Beneath: One woman's Deliverance from a Luciferian Gospel, Mishell McCumber, Page 65.

Those in this movement have intentions of rewriting Christianity, and they can't have Bible-believing Christians get in the way. I also want to point out here that those in the Mystical Miracle Movement believe in opening portals, seeing angel orbs, fire tunnels, calling down fire from heaven, and even spirit travel.

None of this is from God, and people who do these things are truly serving Lucifer.

I want to point out a quote from *"A Final Quest,"* a book written by Rick Joyner: *"Let us understand. The Lord wants us to ascend to Heaven; He wants us to sit on the mount of the assembly; He wants us to be raised above the heights of the clouds, and He wants us to be like Him."* (The View Beneath: One woman's Deliverance from a Luciferian Gospel, Mishell McCumber, Page 119.)

Is this true? Does God really want that for us, or does that sound strangely familiar to what got a certain cherub in Heaven kicked out? In scripture, Lucifer has five "I wills" mentioned.

(Isaiah 14:13-15) *I will ascend into Heaven; I will exalt my throne above the stars of God; I will sit on the mount of the assembly; I will ascend above the heights of the clouds; I will be like the Most High!*

It always goes back to Genesis. The offer is always, *"You can be as gods."*

I am starting to believe that many of these leaders are not only deceived but are the deceivers. It is a well-known fact that Rick Joyner is a Knights of Malta member, and leaders such as him and Bill Johnson conduct ceremonies where they are "knighting" people as a sort of initiation. I ask you, where in the Bible is this mentioned?

In Mishel McCumbers's book, *The View Beneath,* she tells of initiations at church that coincide with occult dates. In her book, she speaks of ringing in the New Year at church, which she now believes was mass ritual to invoke the "Christ spirit," AKA Lucifer, the light bringer.

"Bob Jones—a prophet in Joyner's church—spoke about the King of Glory coming in. The goal was to role play Adam's coming transformation to Godhood, which they believe would occur when the shekinah returns to the temple, activating the inactive part of our DNA. They believe that Christ will indwell His church and will reign on earth as "corporate Christ" or "Christ spirit." It will be a mystical alchemical union that will result in transfiguration; a change that glorifies and exalts man to Godhood." (The View Beneath: One

woman's Deliverance from a Luciferian Gospel, Mishell McCumber, Page 209.)

The occult believes that there is DNA that is inactivated and is preventing us from becoming gods. This is ultimately what every esoteric doctrine points to.

Mishel McCumber, in *"The View Beneath,"* tells of a woman named Cynthia, who was a nanny to the Joyner family, who discovers a Luciferian invitation sitting on their table. Now, Rick Joyner and his wife, Julie, were obsessed with a place called Moravian Falls. As Julie was getting ready one evening, Cynthia thought her attire seemed rather out of character.

"Cynthia told Julie she thought it was beautiful but asked where she planned on wearing it. Julie smiled sweetly and motioned toward an invitation on the table. Cynthia looked at the card and was shocked to find it contained an invitation for Rick and Julie to be initiated into the Luciferian Light." (The View Beneath: One woman's Deliverance from a Luciferian Gospel, Mishell McCumber, Page 141.)

When the Joyners were questioned about this, they stated it wasn't what naysayers thought, and it had nothing to do with Satan but only meant "knowledge, light, and illumination."

This paints an interesting picture of the name "Morningstar Ministries." The name Lucifer can be translated into "morning star." I firmly believe that the occult is infiltrating the church and is on its way to deceive many through the false signs and wonders that the Bible warned us about.

(Mark 13:22) For false christs and false prophets will rise and show signs and wonders to deceive, if possible, even the elect.

Jesus warns more about deception being a sign of the times than anything else. Everything will need to pass through the lens of scripture as these last days draw near.

The New Apostolic Reformation is a movement that seeks to change the face of Christianity by joining all denominations into forms of mysticism while being headed by end-time apostles and prophets.

Let's take a brief look at what the Bible teaches about the five-fold ministry and if it's still for today. The five-fold ministry is laid out in Ephesians 4.

(Ephesians 4:11) And He Himself gave some to be apostles, some prophets, some evangelists, and some pastors and teachers...

The problem happens when one single verse in scripture is isolated and whole doctrines are created from it. Scripture must interpret scripture, so many areas need to be examined. True Biblical apostles were uniquely appointed as eyewitnesses of Jesus' resurrection. Jesus chose each one individually and personally. Seeing the resurrected Christ was a requirement for being an apostle, and Paul understood this.

(Corinthians 15:6-8) After that He was seen by over five hundred brethren at once, of whom the greater part remain to the present, but some have fallen asleep. After that He was seen by James, then by all the apostles. Then last of all He was seen by me also, as by one born out of due time.

Here, Paul seems to refer to himself as the last apostle commissioned by Jesus. Even though Ephesians 4 is used to defend modern day apostles and prophets, Ephesians 2 needs to be read into the equation.

(Ephesians 2:20-21) having been built on the foundation of the apostles and prophets, Jesus Christ Himself being the chief cornerstone, in whom the whole building, being fitted together, grows into a holy temple in the Lord.

The apostles and prophets are listed as the foundation of the building up of the church. The New Apostolic Reformation is trying to lay another foundation, *other than Christ Jesus.* Jesus is the cornerstone because the whole of scripture is pointing to Him throughout time. The apostles and prophets lay the foundation.

(1 Corinthians 3:11) For no other foundation can anyone lay than that which is laid, which is Jesus Christ.

Whatever man tries to build his spirit life upon will be tested. Adding something new to the very foundation of Christianity is evil at its core. It is more important than ever to know and study scripture. NAR is a virus that is having worldwide impact.

Many in this movement use phrases such as "apostles; prophets; destiny; the presence; the glory; revival fire; unity; awakening; five-fold ministry; portals; visionary; generals of the faith; fire-starter; influence; dominion; kingdom now; architect; spiritual mapping; strategic level warfare; spirit of religion; or an unhealthy obsession with accusing people of having a spirit of Jezebel, Leviathan, Ahab, etc." In fact, many coming out of these movements either go completely New Age or end up walking away from their faith forever.

CHAPTER 12
JESUS OF THE NEW AGE

(Matthew 7:13)
Enter by the narrow gate; for wide is the gate and
broad is the way that leads to destruction,
and there are many who go in by it.

I always knew there was a God, and I spent most of my life looking for Him. I was on a journey that was showing me the path to life amidst all the deception. My feet were being firmly planted on a narrow path, proof that God had really been searching for me. My journey to finding Jesus has been a path wrought with pain and heartache. Nobody likes to be lied to, but so few want the truth.

Deep in my heart I wanted the truth, but nothing could have prepared me for what I would encounter. There can only be one truth, and that truth is alive and active within the pages of the Holy Bible. Scripture is literally God-breathed by His own Spirit and handed down to chosen men. However, the world will always try to twist the truth and stop you from believing it.

As you read this chapter, I ask that you read God's word for yourself and in context. It is profound and has the power to change your life.

I do not care if you are a Christian or a non-believer; I fear for what you may encounter and accept as *"truth."* The Bible warned of much deception to arise and that many would fall for a great delusion. I believe we are in those times now. When Jesus' disciples asked Him what to look for prior to His second coming, He warned of deception more than anything else:

(Matthew 24:3-5) Now, as He sat on the Mount of Olives, the disciples came to Him privately, saying, "Tell us, when will these things be? And what will be the sign of Your coming and of the end of the age?" And Jesus answered and said to them: "Take heed that no one deceives you. For many will come in My name, saying, 'I am the Christ,' and will deceive many.

Timothy warns us, *(1 Timothy 4:1) Now the Spirit expressly says that in latter times some will depart from the faith, giving heed to deceiving spirits and doctrines of demons,*

And Matthew says, *(Matthew 24:11) Then many false prophets will rise up and deceive many.*

These Biblical warnings ought to be taken seriously. Satan, the ruler of this earth, isn't afraid of religion or even the veneer of false love and light. He is afraid of *truth*... because it is the truth that will set you free. Every aspect of this life is temporary, so the devil's tactic is to get you to set your eyes on this world. Focus on love, light, unity, and all your carnal desires. If you are focused on what is fleeting, you will forget the fast-approaching guarantee of death.

(2 Corinthians 4:18) While we do not look at the things which are seen but at the things which are not seen. For the things which are seen are temporary, but the things which are not seen are eternal.

There is a worldwide movement taking place, a one-world spirituality that seeks to bind us all: the Christ within, the awakening of man's own divinity.

According to many New Agers and occultists, we are now entering a paradigm shift, an evolved, unified consciousness. We are entering the age of Aquarius. In astrology, this is the very last age we enter. Aquarius is the water bearer, also known as the "coming one."

"Many occultists have long heralded the Aquarian age as a time that would be unparalleled throughout the course of human history... The age of Aquarius is when we are all supposed to realize

that man is God." (A Time of Departing: How Ancient Mystical Practices are Uniting Christians with the World's Religions, Ray Yungen, Page. 134.)

This is the time to bring about a global consciousness. Occultist Dion Fortune said, *"Shifting the consciousness is the key to all occult training." (Lords of Light: The Path of Initiation in the Western Mysteries, W.E. Butler, Page 74)*

My time in the New Age was largely defined by mysticism, which is occultism wrapped in a prettier package.

"Occultism (New Ageism) is defined as the science of mystical evolution; it is the employment of the hidden (i.e. occult) mystical faculties of man to discern the hidden reality of nature; i.e., to see God as the all in all." (A Time of Departing: How Ancient Mystical Practices are Uniting Christians with the World's Religions, Ray Yungen, Page. 147.)

A huge component of occultism is an altered state of consciousness. That is the dividing line between true Christianity and what is part of the kingdom of darkness.

God commands that we are to remain "sober-minded." The Lord gives us reason and intellectual ability for a purpose. God never requires altered states of consciousness as a conduit to reach Him. The bridge to Him was through His shed son's blood upon the cross.

It is then that the veil gets torn, and God is nearer than near and can hear even our simple prayer before it is asked. However, it has now become mainstream to "go within" through meditative, and silent contemplative practices.

While following New Age thought, I always saw Jesus as a special, enlightened individual. He was even mentioned by New Age teachers, so it falsely lulled me into deceit. Due to my Biblical illiteracy, I never understood that there was a false Jesus, an imposter.

My excitement would grow as I watched spirituality come more into the limelight of mainstream media. I've always been very spiritual, and I was keenly aware of how spirituality was being linked on popular TV programs, college campuses, and even certain practices being touted as scientific.

I could see a paradigm shift happening all around me. During my time in yoga and meditation, I *felt* closer to God. I experienced peace, like a drug. This is what would get me hooked. I would watch people, such as late Dr. Wayne Dywer on Oprah network, and see the people on her Super Soul Sunday television show who were, in fact, helping sell the masses a renewed spirituality. I had no idea how exclusive Jesus would become and how all of this was deception.

There is a universal one-world Christ that will arise and unite all religions. Popular New Age proponents have spread this message on TV while their self-help books fill the bookshelves, often becoming national best sellers. Many of these books have authors that have written channelled messages from a divine being, claiming new revelation or twisting what is already written in Holy scripture.

Helen Schucman heard an inner voice that claimed to be "Jesus."

Barabara Marx Hubbard heard an inner voice that claimed to be "Christ."

Neale Donald Walsch heard an inner voice that claimed to be God. (*False Christ Coming: Does Anybody Care? Warren B. Smith, Section 1148, Paragraph 1.*)

A new gospel is being preached, and that is the gospel of the New Age Christ. During my World Religion class in college we learned about some of the newest religious movements. One of these movements happened to be outlined in the book, *"A Course in Miracles,"* by Marianne Williamson. This book claimed to be the foundation for inner peace, containing a curriculum which claims to assist its readers in achieving spiritual transformation. This book was channelled writing and was a spiritual movement, not simply a book.

Marianne Williamson, co-founder of the Global Renaissance Alliance, one day, heard a voice that said, "This is a course in miracles, please take notes." Marianne even appeared on the Oprah Winfrey show to tell her story.

"The Global Renaissance Alliance became the Peace Alliance in 2005 and describes itself as a "citizen-based network of spiritual activists," whose mission is to make a stand in our local and national communities; for the role of the spiritual principle is the New Age notion that we are all part of God." (False Christ Coming: Does Anybody Care? by Warren B. Smith, Section 1445.)

In *"Healing of the Soul,"* also by Williamson, she writes: *"According to the mystical traditions, God carries this plan within His mind, seeking always, in every way, channels for its furtherance. His plan for the evolution of humanity, and the preparation of teachers to guide it, is called within the esoteric traditions of great work." (False Christ Coming: Does Anybody Care? by Warren B. Smith, Section 1463, Paragraph 2.)*

Esoteric equals occult. The occult is secret, hidden knowledge that is forbidden in the Bible. The occult is taking over every facet of society, and Christians are lacking the knowledge to follow truth. This esoteric knowledge is the same apple that Eve bit into: the promise of the knowledge of good and evil. *"You shall be as gods."*

All the ancient mystery schools are holders of esoteric (hidden) knowledge. It is usually accomplished by some sort of mystical technique that opens one up to the spiritual world. It requires initiations and levels.

"What was kept secret or hidden? It can best be summed up as the knowledge of the laws and forces that underlie the universe but are not evident to the five senses of man's normal perception. Basically, they taught an awareness of the invisible worlds for wisdom and guidance and the development of psychic abilities and spiritual healing techniques." (Alice Bailey: Mother of the New Age Movement, Ray Yungun, Section 48, Paragraph 2)

In the Bible, the occult and its techniques for hidden wisdom and power are forbidden. God hides nothing. God made one way to connect with Him, and that is through His son, Jesus Christ, who became a ransom for many *(Mark 10:45)*. This is what makes

Christianity vastly different from other religions. Other religions are based on man *doing and attaining,* whereas, with Jesus, *IT IS DONE AND FINISHED.* As a Christian, we can never attain divinity this side of heaven; we must, instead, become less, so He (Jesus) can become greater *(John 3:30).*

The Christian church is no longer separate from the occult but is becoming one. In certain charismatic sects of Christianity, it is believed that we can perform the same miracles as Jesus. The ancient mystery schools all echo the same teaching...

"Happy and blessed one, you have become divine instead of mortal" *(Alice Bailey: Mother of the New Age Movement, Ray Yungun, Section 48, Paragraph 4)*

Alice Bailey was a famous occultist who taught long ago that, during this Age of Aquarius, the world would be awaiting a healer and Savior of mankind. This Savior would unite all mankind under his guidance. Bailey used the term, "The coming one."

While Christians wait for the second coming of Jesus, the "coming one" would embody all great religions and principles of occultism.

"The coming one will not be a Buddhist, not an American, Jew, Italian, or Russian—his title is not important; he is for all humanity, to unite all religions, philosophies, and nations." (Alice Bailey: Mother of the New Age Movement, Ray Yungun, Section 125, Paragraph 1.)

Alice Bailey prophesied many things to come. When the Bible speaks of a great falling away, I believe that falling away is following another "Jesus."

Alice Bailey spoke of a "regeneration of the churches." Christianity is one of the largest religions there is. The occult is not going to go against the church but, instead, go through the church, as a catalyst to merging all faiths. *"The Christian church in its many branches can serve as a St. John the Baptist, as a voice crying in the wilderness, and as a nucleus through which world illumination may be accomplished,"* (Alice Bailey: Mother of the New Age Movement, Ray Yungun, Section 156, Paragraph 2.)

In 2 Thessalonians, chapter 2, Paul proclaims that they will fall away to "the mystery of lawlessness." *(2 Thessalonians 2:7)*

For the mystery of lawlessness is already at work; only He who now restrains will do so until He is taken out of the way.

In Greek, the word "mystery," used in the context of evil, means hidden, or occult. The church is still using Christian lingo on the outside but has changed to contemplative spirituality on the inside. Instead of knowing God on a rational level or through Biblical theology, we now have "experiential faith."

"This feeling can be associated with spiritual realities, and I believe it can be manipulated to that end, acting as a doorway into supernatural realms. Unchecked or intentionally pursuing such a state of being as a spiritual condition, I contest, and others have argued, can be psychologically disrupting and spiritually deceptive." (Game of Gods, Carl Teichrib, Page 393.)

This has been my own experience thus far. Whether seeking experiences in the New Age or seeking the supernatural in a church, I was unknowingly opening myself up to supernatural realms that God had no intention of us accessing. Instead of emptying our minds, God requires of us to fill our minds on what is good and acceptable in His sight. It is an action, not a passive state.

(Philippians 4:8) *Finally, brethren, whatever things are true, whatever things are noble, whatever things are just, whatever things are pure, whatever things are lovely, whatever things are of good report, if there is any virtue and if there is anything praiseworthy—meditate on these things.*

The West has moved away from Biblical ideas, and all contemplative practices have been pulled in from Eastern spirituality. These Eastern philosophies are melding with Christianity. God has called us to be a separate people.

As Carl Teichrib writes in *"Game of Gods"; "Interfaithism undermines the truth claim of Jesus Christ. He can only be another moral teacher or spiritual reformer, nothing more... If all faiths are equally valid expressions of truth, then none of them are." (Game of Gods, Carl Teicrib, Page 411.)*

When I was in the New Age and had a kundalini awakening, it was often taught that this power is dormant and required "activation." So how does one activate? Well, simply put, by an altered state of consciousness. The samadhi of yoga, and later ecstatic worship in a charismatic church, conjured up the same feelings and spiritual intoxication. This is universal energy, found in the sufi swirling dervishes, and contemplative prayer practices, as well as using psychedelic substances.

The Christian church has become one with the New Age. It no longer stands on the written Word of God, but, instead, on the sinking sand of experiential faith. We are living in perilous times, yet why is the church remaining silent and refusing to warn about counterfeit spirituality taking place? The New Apostolic Reformation has polluted churches and filled them with mysticism. It has become a giant cult-like environment. Churches are led astray by guru-like men who call themselves "apostles," and "prophets," but espouse new revelation to their congregations.

Many have chosen to walk in the "prophetic," seeking after signs and miracles with a desire that is unquenchable. The Holy Spirit has become a force that must be activated, with conferences selling an "experience with God," or what's known as, "Holy Spirit activation." Many church goers are being told that "God is doing a new thing" and He's "filling us with new wine." God's people have become so intoxicated, they have lost all discernment.

The Holy Spirit is known as an equal member of the Godhead. A person, not a force as in the New Age ideologies. What's interesting is the prophet Daniel makes mention of the God of "forces" in conjunction with the antichrist, *(Daniel 11:38)*. Leaders of the New Age/new gospel ask, "What if I am not a 'man' at all, but rather a force?"

The "Christ" of a *"Course in Miracles,"* by Helen Schucman, states that there is *"an irresistible force"* within each person.

Marianne Williamson, in *"Inspiring Teachings on A Course in Miracles,"* explains that this "universal force" can be activated within each person and has the "power to make all things right."

The New Age Christ tells Barabara Marx Hubbard that on the day of "planetary Pentecost," a "planetary smile" will flash across the face of mankind; that an "uncontrollable joy," that is described as "the joy of the force," will ripple through the one body of humanity.

Benjamin Crème describes the event as a "Pentecostal experience for all."

The 'Christ' of "*A Course in Miracles,*" tells how the world ends in *"peace and laughter." (False Christ Coming: Does Anybody Care? Warren B. Smith, Section 2400, Paragraph 1.)*

A good question to ask is this: Is the "force" that New Agers and occultists describe the same "force" that is eagerly welcomed within the church as "revival"?

In chapter 11, we discussed how the NAR is made up of different streams that originated from the Toronto Blessing. This "revival" gave way to strange phenomenon such as "Holy laughter," being "drunk in the Spirit," making animal sounds, and people describing a burning sensation felt throughout their bodies. None of this is Biblical but occurs in all different forms of mystical traditions.

I have heard Christians defend "holy laughter" as "the joy of the Lord." Is it only coincidence that Barbara Marx Hubbard's planetary Pentecost is known as 'the joy of the force" or "planetary smile"?

After all, many occultists have predicted the coming one and the regeneration of the church. It's interesting that the New Apostolic Reformation in the church is doing just that: reforming the church and making it based on experiential faith. Bethel Church, in Redding, California, serves as a mecca for the new reform that is happening in churches.

Nothing makes this clearer than the book, "*Physics of Heaven,*" where *a* group of evangelical Christian leaders introduce the New Age as something that has been stolen from us (Christians) that we must redeem. Bill Johnson is the head pastor of Bethel, Redding, and he and his wife wrote excerpts in this book. He considers himself an apostle, and one who has been specially shown new revelation for the Body of Christ. This book is filled with New Age ideas, and their ministry is serving as a vehicle to import this poison to various churches on a global level.

Kris Vallotton, from Bethel Church, writes the foreword for *"Physics of Heaven."* According to this so-called prophet, *"This book reads like a journal that emerged from a Holy Spirit think tank where great, spiritual leaders gathered to discuss their insights into the complexities of God. Through their collective intelligence, these seers have emerged with new perspectives never before pondered."* (Physics of Heaven, Judy Franklin, and Ellyn Davis, Section 85.)

Really? *New perspectives never before pondered?* Is the cannon of scripture not complete? From the old testament through the new testament, God's revelation and plan has been revealed through His son, Jesus. As I've said before, the Bible states, *"There's nothing new under the sun,"* **(Ecclesiastes 1:9)**. However, according to *"The Physics of Heaven,"* God is up to something new—something that will transform us at the deepest level of who we are and will be ushered in by a new form of sound or vibration." How exactly will this come to be?

According to Bob Jones (a well-known false prophet), he shares in this book that, *"God is beginning to "breathe" on His people again to prepare us for a second Pentecost that tunes us and brings us into harmony with God."* (Physics of Heaven, Judy Franklin, and Ellyn Davis Section 21.)

Just like the occultists, these Christian leaders also believe we are about to experience another Pentecost. *"I believe we are on the verge of experiencing Pentecost on a new level and in a new measure. Time and again the prophets have declared that "something is coming," and our hearts are filled with expectation to receive all that God has for us. We still await the fullness of what we know is possible in God—a fullness of Pentecost, for which the original Pentecost provided the down payment."* (Physics of Heaven, Judy Franklin, and Ellyn Davis Section 95.)

In the Bible, "Pentecost" was a historical event that is recorded in Acts 2. This event was signalling a new era in God dealing with His people. In the Old Testament, the Holy Spirit only came upon people at certain moments; whereas, now, the claim is that the Holy Spirit is permanently indwelling God's people for them to now witness throughout the world. The Day of

Pentecost was a one-time event, not one that would need to be repeated in the future. Once indwelt with the Holy Spirit, what more can be given to you?

The occult likes to take what is Biblical and twist it to fit its own agenda. Many Christians have begun to experience occult bodily manifestations.

In chapter 14 of "*The Physics of Heaven,*" it states, "*Many men and women of God have experienced physical shaking and vibrating and seen bright light when undergoing a deep spiritual transformation. Others have described sensations like electric shocks when encountering God's presence*" (Physics of Heaven, Judy Franklin, and Ellyn Davis Section 147.)

Pastor Bill Johnson describes his experience as "*Unimaginable power began to surge through my body. If I had been plugged into a wall socket with a thousand volts of electricity flowing through my body, I can't imagine it would have been much different... My arms and legs shot out in silent explosions as this power was released through my hands and feet. The more I tried to stop it, the worse it got.*"

Bill's wife, Beni Johnson, had something of a similar experience. After a church meeting one night, Beni describes, "*There were people laid out all over the floor, laughing and having all kinds of physical manifestations... I noticed a very inebriated man staggering around, touching people. This man was drunk in the Spirit... When he touched me with his finger, a holy current went right through me. When it touched me, I began to shake violently... I had absolutely no control over my body. I knew it was God,*" (Physics of Heaven, Judy Franklin, and Ellyn Davis Section 153.)

Was this really God, though? You won't find these types of manifestations in the Bible, but you will find them in the occult and kundalini cults. I believe that what I experienced in the New Age and the charismatic church were both the same occult energy. In fact, what both Beni and Bill Johnson describe is identical to what yoga enthusiasts refer to as "energy awakenings" resulting from kundalini.

Let's look at some people describing kundalini awakenings. Both of the following are from the "Themindfulword.org" website.

The article is entitled, *"Kundalini Awakening Experiences: 3 stories of intense and sudden energetic transformation."*

Kimberly describes that she, *"Suddenly felt she couldn't move her body or open her eyes."* She felt heat and bright light around her body... Over the next few days, she had a feeling of *"energy rising through my body with a loud screeching sound."* She saw visions of colors and symbols.

Simon describes, *"Shooting pains and convulsions of energy going up and down his spine,"* and he had, *"The clearest understanding of God and the universe."*

Just like Bill Johnson, many others have these same experiences while not being Christians. Many who share these experiences of "God" can go on to believe in the interconnectedness of us all. It is opposite Christianity and is pantheism. Pantheism is the belief that God consists of everyone and everything. For example, a tree is God, a mountain is God, the universe is God, all people are God. It is these types of beliefs that will unite us all and enable us to accept the "coming one."

Perhaps this all sounds crazy to you, but much of what goes on in this world happens openly, in plain sight. Jesus said while here on earth that the reason He was hated was because, *(John 7:7), The world cannot hate you, but it hates Me because I testify of it that its works are evil.*

He also described the devil as *"the ruler of this earth."*

(John 12:31) now the ruler of this world will be cast out.

We as Christians have been born again, made as new creations covered by the blood of Jesus, with a new heart and eyes to see. Jesus is exclusive from any other religion, yet every other religion needs to account for Him in some way. They do this by denying His divinity and His truth claims. This "coming one" is a savior that will appear on earth, bringing a false peace and bringing a one-world religion.

As I explained previously, occultists have had an agenda since the beginning of time, only now it is coming together quickly and succinctly.

For instance, did you know there is a world foundation, called The Lucis Trust, that serves as the spiritual foundation of the United Nations? This spiritual foundation was created by famous occultist, Alice Bailey, who has written many books through Lucis Publishing Company.

The Lucis Trust was established in 1922 to *"foster recognition of the universal spiritual principles at the heart of all work to build right relations,"* according to their website. Lucis Trust was incorporated into the United Kingdom in 1935. Initially, it had a publishing company called Lucifer Publishing Company. "Lucifer" is seen here as "the angel who brought light to the world." However, because some Christians identified Lucifer with Satan, the name was changed to Lucis Publishing Company.

So, here is the realization that the entire world has its principles largely built on the occult and is totally opposed to Biblical truths.

Alice Bailey started a school for occult philosophy in 1923, called the Arcane School. People can actually join the school and learn occult principles. They have a spiritual hierarchy that serves to implement a "plan."

"The spiritual hierarchy works through three major aspects or "departments" of work. The Department of Government, the Department of Religion, and the Department of Education, with its subsidiary aspects of science, philosophy, psychology, and culture and the arts... Therefore, these disciples preparing for active service to the hierarchy find their place within seven major areas of human life... By building of clear, plan-imbued thoughtforms, through the technique of occult meditation." (lucistrust.org website.)

Here is where I start to connect the dots. Yoga and meditation practices have grown and expanded to every area of life. This is not coincidence. Next, what I experienced in a NAR church is what is known as Dominionism, or the Seven-mountain Mandate.

Now, what these churches are teaching is that we (Christians) have a mandate by God to take back the seven spheres of society. These seven mountains, or spheres, are business, government, family, religion, media, education, and entertainment. The Lucis

Trust statement above also mentions *seven* areas of human life that need to be taken over. Religion, education, science, philosophy, culture and the arts. Very similar goals to Christian Kingdom Now theology.

Lucis Trust has what is known as, "New Group World Servers." These are, *"Men of goodwill who co-operate to form part of the new group of world servers which is working to implement the plan." (The New Group of world servers, Lucistrust.org, Paragraph 3.)*

This hierarchy, *"Directs world events so that evolving conscious-ness may express itself through adequate social, political, religious and economic forms (The Spiritual Hierarchy, Alice Bailey, Lucistrust.org.)*

I also want to mention here that this hierarchy receives an esoteric "fire of God," according to the Lucis Trust website. Interesting that many churches have become experience based and often call down the "fire of God." The ultimate "plan" of this esoteric hierarchy is a one-world religion and one-world government.

The Lucis trust is built on occult principles and not only speaks of a world religion but a coming one, who will be bringing the kingdom of heaven to earth and implementing a bigger, greater world Pentecost experience. Along the same lines, many in NAR churches are moving from doctrine to experiential faith and unity of denominations. People in the NAR camps also speak of ush-ering the kingdom of God to earth, so that 'Christ' can return.

According to writings by Alice Bailey of the coming world hierarchy, *"People are moving out from under doctrinal authority into direct, personal, and spiritual experience; they are coming under direct authority which contact with Christ and His disciples, the masters, ever confer" (Ponder on This, Alice Bailey, page 166).*

Regarding the Kingdom of God, the Lucis Trust website states, *"The bringing in of the Kingdom of God, the preparation for the coming 'Christ' and salvaging of humanity demand courage, organization, business acumen, psychology, and persistence."*

It's quite interesting that the plans are almost identical to that of the new Mystical Miracle Movement of the NAR churches.

The Luciferian agenda is too smart to go against the church but, instead, will merge with the church in grand deception.

Lucis Trust speaks plainly of the coming world religion. Its agenda and plan are not hidden but there for all to see.

"There will be the invocative work of the masses of people every-where, trained by the spiritually-minded people of the world (working in the churches whenever possible, under enlightened clergy) to accept the fact of the approaching spiritual energies, focused through 'Christ' and His spiritual hierarchy." (The Reappearance of the Christ, Alice Bailey, Chapter 6, Paragraph 39, lucistrust.org.)

They clearly have those that are working for their agenda to change the state of the churches and get their eyes off Biblical doctrine. It will need to be a spiritual evolution of man. Instead of the Book of Revelation, which declares the return and final reign of Jesus Christ and destroying His enemies, it is going to be a world-savior figure that will unite all and bring peace on earth. *This savior that is being anticipated is none other than the anti-Christ.*

(Revelation 13:13-15) *He performs great signs, so that he even makes fire come down from heaven on the earth in the sight of men. And he deceives those who dwell on the earth by those signs which he was granted to do in the sight of the beast, telling those who dwell on the earth to make an image to the beast who was wounded by the sword and lived. He was granted power to give breath to the image of the beast, that the image of the beast should both speak and cause as many as would not worship the image of the beast to be killed.*

(Daniel 8:24-25) *And his power shall be mighty, but not by his own power: he shall destroy wonderfully, and shall prosper, and practice, and shall destroy the mighty and the holy people...he shall magnify himself in his heart, and by **peace** he will destroy many.*

The Bible speaks of a rapture. Those truly belonging to God will be taken off this earth before the rule and reign of the anti-Christ, who will sit in the synagogue and be worshipped as God by all the world.

(2 Thessalonians 2:4) He will oppose and will exalt himself over everything that is called God or is worshipped so that he sets himself up in God's temple, proclaiming to be God.

In both the occult and the Christian New Apostolic Reformation, those pesky Bible-believing Christians will need to be "removed" from the earth.

Barbara Marx Hubbard wrote a book called *"Revelation: Our Crisis is a Birth."* In this book, Hubbard rewrites the Book of Revelation. Instead of a violent Armageddon, humanity can have a more positive future and *"openly declare its oneness with him and all creation."* It explains us awakening to our own divinity and evolving to have a planetary birth experience.

According to Hubbard's "Christ," there will be a selection process. *"Christ states that those who see themselves as separate and not divine, hinder humanity's ability to spiritually evolve. Those who deny their own divinity are like cancer cells in the body of God. Cancer cells must be healed or completely removed from the body. This removal is by the "selection process." The "selection process" results in the deaths of those who refuse to see themselves as part of God." (False Christ Coming: Does Anybody Care? Warren B. Smith, Section 505.)*

Now compare this to Christian leader, Rick Joyner, of Morning Star Ministries. He teaches his congregation that there are two different camps. One being the "blues," and one being the "grays."

Rick Joyner believes that these two will need to battle it out. *"Like the ocean and sky, the blues stood for revelation, expanse, spiritual enlightenment, and openness of spirit—a new breed. The grays represented the brain-logical reasoning. They clung to doctrine and scripture instead of progressive revelation. The grays would need to be overcome and destroyed in the fight for the true church to evolve to the next level." (The View Beneath, Mishel McCumber, Page 65.)*

So, both the occult and the New Apostolic Reformation believe in ushering in a Christ-like figure to take dominion of the world. Both are awaiting an epic second world Pentecost. This will ensure man discovering his own divinity. This is not from God. This is the New-Age "Christ consciousness," the God within.

Remember, this is the very same lie whispered in the Garden of Eden by the serpent. Both the New Age movement and NAR speak of removing those who refuse to "evolve." However, biblically speaking, these will be the true saints of God that stick to God's truth, some even unto death.

The Bible warns continually about deception:

(Colossians 2:8) Beware lest anyone cheat you through philosophy and empty deceit, according to the tradition of men, according to the basic principles of the world, and not according to Christ.

(1 Timothy 4:1) Now the Spirit expressly says that in later times some will depart from the faith, giving heed to deceiving spirits and doctrines of demons.

(2 Timothy 3:13) But evil men and imposters will grow worse and worse, deceiving and being deceived.

(John 14:6) Jesus said to him, "I am the way, the truth, and the life. No one comes to the Father except through me.

(John 17:17) Sanctify them by your truth. Your word is truth.

Truth in this world has become a subjective concept, but truth, by very definition, is "That which is true or in accordance with fact or reality." Truth will stand the test of time and always come to the surface if searched for. Truth does not care about one's opinion or feelings.

I have always been a truth seeker, no matter the cost. I didn't want only what I desired to believe but what was *truth*. I embarked on a journey of finding the light surrounded by darkness. I was led to the narrow path of life. My aching soul was quenched by the Living Water of Jesus.

Jesus is the way, the truth and the life. The evil I encountered when involved with New Age and kundalini awakening didn't succeed in overtaking me only because of the grace of God. Jesus was revealing to me what lied behind the darkness that is masquerading as light.

(Luke 11:35) Therefore take heed that the light which is in you is not darkness.

I write this book not to judge anyone but out of love and deep concern. I ask you to question what the truth really is in this world. I ask you to research everything and pray to Jesus to reveal himself to you with an open heart.

And, if you are a Christian, I ask you to search the scriptures and be aware of the occult and mystical traditions creeping into churches everywhere. Seek truth, and, above all, stand for the truth and ask God to protect you from deception.

I have only begun to scratch the surface of how deep a rabbit hole this is. I hope by reading this a few seeds have been planted and an awareness has begun to take root.

CONCLUSION

THE NARROW PATH

CHAPTER 13
NEXT STEPS

If you are wondering where to turn at this point, I ask you to start with a simple prayer to Jesus and begin by reading scripture daily. As far as denominations go, I'm not here to tell you what works best. However, it is imperative (albeit hard to find in these times) to be a part of a Bible believing church, one that teaches expository Bible messages. "Expository preaching" is preaching that details the meaning of a particular text or passage of Scripture. It explains what the Bible means by what it says—without hype and emotionalism.

I would advise to stay away from prosperity-type preachers who teach about your destiny instead of how to die to yourself. As previously stated, there is a rise of a global church, presenting with signs and wonders instead of the simple gospel. These are New Apostolic Reformation churches, and usually are led by false apostles and prophets. I know this can be a tough road to navigate, but I want you to know I'm not the only one out there with these stories and experiences.

I have met many others along the way who have encountered frightening kundalini awakenings, either in the church or from yoga/meditation. Many ex-New Agers are coming to know Jesus Christ as the way, the life, and the truth.

A good friend of mine, Doreen Virtue, was a famous New Age author and psychic medium, known by her angel cards and readings. She is now a born-again Christian, and her testimony is on YouTube. She and another friend have an excellent Facebook group for those who are coming out of these movements and are searching for truth. This group is called "From New Age to Christianity Recovery Group."

I, as well, have a Facebook group called "The Narrow Path" that is linked to this book.

A wonderful book that I highly recommend and is exhaustive in its research of the New Age and the political/scientific agenda of the one-world religion is "*Game of Gods: The Temple of Man in the Age of Re-Enchantment,*" by Carl Teicrib. He has sat in on many World Parliament of Religion, and United Nations meetings and agendas. He has also attended well-known Burning Man events and witnessed how these all play out as a social and political experiment to promote a vision of global unity, all while being hostile to Christianity.

The point I would really like to drive home at this point is who Jesus is. First and foremost, Jesus wasn't simply a man. Jesus was fully man and fully God. The common thread you will see with false religions and even Christian cults is that they downplay His divinity while elevating man. In many church pulpits today, a different Jesus is being preached. The emphasis is on how we can perform the same miracles as Jesus, if not greater than what He did.

Often in the Bible, Jesus, after performing miracles, would tell His disciples, "See to it that no one knows about this." Jesus wanted less focus on miracles performed and more on the message of salvation.

Jesus asked His disciples a very important question: *(Matthew 16:13-20, Mark 8:27-30, and John 6:66-71) "Who do you say I am?"* His disciples answered by saying, *"Some say John the Baptist, others say Elijah, and still others that a prophet of old has risen."*

But then Jesus repeats the question. This time Peter replies, *"The Christ, son of the living God"*

Others in the world had the wrong answer. Like today, other religions believe He was an ascended master, a prophet, or merely a great teacher, here to teach you to access your own divinity.

But only those closest to Him know the correct answer. He is God in the flesh. He was the promised Messiah. Jesus responds to His disciples: *"Blessed are you, for this was not revealed to you by flesh and blood, but by my Father in heaven."*

Jesus was the literal Holy Word manifested. The entire Old Testament was Jesus concealed, while the New testament is Jesus revealed. Jesus came as the final sacrifice for sin and to defeat death on a cross so we could, one day, walk in the garden with God again. He gave us eternal life after death. He did not come to turn us into godmen.

What the New Age/occult/mysticism seek to do, is teach us to access our own divinity. We can attain power and live by our own will. An outside God is not needed. What is popular in NAR churches and amongst people such as Bill Johnson, is the belief that we too can attain all that Jesus is. They chase signs, wonders, and revival, attempting to bring heaven down to earth. Bill Johnson declares right on his Facebook page, *"If Jesus Christ performed His earthly miracles as God, I stand amazed. But if He did them as man dependent on God, I am compelled to follow His lead."* This is essentially denying Jesus' divinity.

Jesus never stopped being God at any moment. He performed these miracles because He was God, not because He was in right standing with God. He wasn't here to teach us what to attain, instead He was here as our Savior. If Jesus only performed miracles as a man, and one we could emulate, then He was no different than any other great teacher.

All other religions teach that we can attain something by doing XYZ. No other leader died for you. If He was only a man, a good teacher, then His entire brutal death and shed blood was for nothing, and completely in vain. See, the price for sin is hell, and we'll never be able to attain enough righteousness to pay that debt. Jesus did things that no man can and literally paid the debt for our sin.

The gospel message is simple. Jesus is the son of God, who went to the cross to offer His life as a sacrificial payment for the guilt of our sins. On the third day He arose from a tomb,

demonstrating God's power over sin and death. That's why Jesus is our Savior, and one day those who have given their lives to Him will also rise to eternal life with the Father.

(1 Corinthians 15:1-7) Moreover, brethren, I declare to you the Gospel which I preached to you, which also you received and in which you stand, by which also you are saved, if you hold fast that word which I preached to you—unless you believed in vain.

For I delivered to you first of all that which I also received: that Christ died for our sins according to the Scriptures, and that He was buried, and that He rose again the third day according to the Scriptures, and that He was seen by Cephas, then by the twelve. After that He was seen by over five hundred brethren at once, of whom the greater part remains to the present, but some have fallen asleep. After that He was seen by James, then by all the apostles.

It is so important that what we believe is truth. I hope this book helped open your mind and gave you things to ponder. I strongly encourage you to do your own research into these topics, and I pray you will seek out God and ask Jesus to reveal himself to you. This has been a journey, and my hope is God will protect and guide you on the narrow path to life.

If you have finished reading this far, I sincerely thank you for taking the time to hear and contemplate my story. I do not think its coincidence that you have been led to my book. My prayer for you is that God is working on your heart and calling you unto Himself. I have been through a lot in these last few years, but I wouldn't trade knowing God for anything, even if it brings me much hardship.

Please do not think I'm judging you in any way. Perhaps you do yoga and argue it's only for the stretching. I'm not here to judge your motives but simply to warn and share my deep personal experiences with spirituality. I'm not even here to tell you not to do yoga but to provide some facts so you can judge and decide for yourself. There is a much bigger paradigm being pushed and presented to the masses than stretching and exercise. There are myriad other forms of exercise that don't carry such a price tag. If you are a Christian, valuing truth above all things marks you, and you should understand how yoga and Eastern spirituality are counter to core-Christian beliefs. I invite you to do your own research and pray to Jesus for answers.

I feel my story and my message are very important to share with the world. I feel Jesus has set me free and delivered me from evil. This book is about warning, not judgement. It would be easier for me to stay quiet and keep my beliefs to myself. However, out of sincere love, I cannot do that. I feel we have approached a time where values and spirituality are changing rapidly, and Bible prophecy is being fulfilled. There is a broad road, and many are traveling that way. I choose the narrow path of truth, and my hope is you will too.

For those readers who are already Christians, I hope this book will make you consider what that really means and what the cost to follow Christ entails. The American church, in many ways, has become about following Jesus for wealth, health and happiness. Many other churches have opened their doors to forms of mysticism and have merged with deceptive practices that are more akin to witchcraft than to Biblical Christianity.

Jesus has a reason for all I've encountered. Being involved with New Age religion and occult techniques has enabled me to pick up on the same practices right in church. It wouldn't be right for me not to warn of the parallels and syncretism going on. So many things that are going on in society and spirituality are preparing us for a new world order with a false peace. Humans cannot organize peace, only Jesus can do that.

(1 Thessalonians 5:3-6) For when they say, "peace and safety!" then sudden destruction comes upon them, as labor pains upon a pregnant woman. And they shall not escape. But you brethren are not in darkness, so this day should not overtake you as a thief. You are all sons of light and sons of the day… Therefore let us not sleep, as others do, but let us watch and be sober.

In *"Game of Gods: The Temple of Man in the Age of Re-enchantment,"* Carl Teicrib writes, *"Where roads intersect, new edifices of religion, politics, technology, and culture are constructed. The Judeo-Christian structures are being dismantled and replaced;*

we are witnessing the creation of a new global neighbourhood. Its builders anticipate a coming synthesis, and oneness becomes the banner under which they work." (Page 1.)

All of this may seem overwhelming to you, but God is not the author of confusion, and I promise if you seek God with your whole heart and study His word and in context, the Holy Spirit will illuminate your path.

(Psalm 119:105) *Your word is a lamp to my feet and a light to my path.*

BIBLIOGRAPHY

-Aletheia, Frater. "Thelemic Yoga: Beginnings of Yoga." Thelemic Union, August 5, 2018. https://thelemicunion.com/ thelemic-yoga-series-pt-1-beginnings-yoga/.

Bailey, Alice. "The Spiritual Hierarchy - World Goodwill (Lucis Trust)." Lucis Trust. Accessed January 22, 2020. https://www. lucistrust.org/world_goodwill/world_goodwill_homepage/ the_spiritual_hierarchy_b

Blavatsky, H. P., and Michael Gomes. *The Secret Doctrine*. Vol. 2. New York: Jeremy P. Tarcher/Penguin, 2009, Pg. 673

Bailey, Alice. "The Reappearance of the Christ (Lucis Trust)." • Lucis Trust. Accessed January 22, 2020. https://www.lucistrust. org/meetings_and_events/three_major_spiritual_festivals/ the_christ_s_festival/the_reappearance_the_christ1.

Bailey, Alice, and Djwhal Khul. *Ponder on This: from the Writings of Alice A. Bailey and the Tibetan Master, Djwhal Khul*. New York, NY: Lucis Pub. Co., 2003, Pg. 166

Brown, Candy Gunther. *The Healing Gods: Complementary and Alternative Medicine in Christian America*. New York: Oxford University Press, 2013, Pg. 134

Butler, W. E., and M. A. Geikie. *Lords of Light: the Path of Initiation in the Western Mysteries: the Teachings of the Ibis Fraternity*. Rochester, VT: Destiny Books, 1990. Pg. 74

Craven, John. "Meditation and Psychotherapy." *The Canadian Journal of Psychiatry*, October 1, 1989. https://journals. sagepub.com/doi/abs/10.1177/070674378903400705.

Crowley, Aleister. *Eight Lectures on Yoga*. United States: CreateSpace Independent Publishing Platform, 2014, Pg. 51

Crowley, Aleister, Mary Desti, Leila Waddell, and Hymenaeus Beta. *Magick: Liber ABA*. Boston, Md: Weiser Books, 1997

Dale, Cyndi. *The Subtle Body: An Encyclopedia of Your Energetic Anatomy*. Boulder, CO: Sounds True, 2009, Pgs, 237, 241, 251, 274

Eliason, GH. *The Generations of the Antichrist An Argument for the Sake of Heaven*. Outskirts Press, 2010, Pg. 33

Farias, Miguel. *The Buddha Pill*. Watkins Publishing, 2019.

FRANKLIN, JUDY DAVIS ELLYN. *PHYSICS OF HEAVEN*. Place of publication not identified: DESTINY IMAGE INCORPORATE, 2016, Pgs, 21, 85, 95, 147, 153

Ford, Michael W. *Liber Hvhi Magick of the Adversary*. Era Horrificus Succubus Publishing, 2005, Pg., 110, 112

Grant, Kara Leah. "A List of Yoga Scandals Involving Gurus, Teachers, Students, Sex, and Other Inappropriate Behavior." Yoga Lunchbox, February 17, 2015. theyogalunchbox.co.nz.

Greyson, Bruce. "The Physio-Kundalini Syndrome and Mental Illness." *The Journal of Transpersonal Psychology*1 (1993). http://www.atpweb.org/jtparchive/trps-25-93-01-043.pdf.

Hilborn, David. "A CHRONOLOGY of the TORONTO BLESSING." Accessed January 22, 2020. http://www.banner. org.uk/media/books/A%20chronicle%20of%20the%20 TB%20by%20David%20Hilborn.pdf

Hunt, Dave. *Yoga and the Body of Christ*. Bend, OR: Berean Call, 2013, Pg. 9

Jung, Carl Gustav. *The Psychology of Kundalini Yoga*. Princeton N.J.: Princeton University Press, 1996, Pg. 30

Jung, C. G., and Jenny L. Yates. *Jung on Death and Immortality*. Princeton, NJ: Princeton University Press, 1999, Pg. 31

Lalich, Janja. "Cult Characteristics." Apologetics Index, December 13, 2017. http://www.apologeticsindex. org/268-characteristics-of-cults.

McCumber, Michelle. *The View Beneath: One Woman's Deliverance from the Luciferian Gospel*. Mighty Roar Books, 2016, Pg. 65, 119, 141, 209

MICHAELSEN, JOHANNA. *The BEAUTIFUL SIDE OF EVIL.* Harvest House Publishers, 1982.

Pirozok, Don. *Kingdom Come: A Biblical Response to Dominion Theology.* Spokane Valley, WA: Pilgrims Progress Publishing, 2016, Pg. 71, 89, 110

Poloma, Margaret. The "Toronto Blessing" and Church Structure, an article by Margaret Poloma. Accessed January 23, 2020. http://hirr.hartsem.edu/research/pentecostalism_polo-maart6.html.

Randles, Bill. *Weighed and Found Wanting: Putting the Toronto Blessing in Context.* Marion, IA: publisher not identified, 1995, Pg. 13

Shapiro, DH. "Adverse Effects Of Meditation: A Preliminary Investigation ..." Accessed January 22, 2020. http://deanehshapirojr.org/wp-content/uploads/2016/10/Adverse-Effect-of-Meditation.pdf.

Jr., William C. Shiel. "Sleep Paralysis Information by MedicineNet.com." MedicineNet. MedicineNet, December 27, 2018. https://www.medicinenet.com/script/main/art.asp?articlekey=9806.

Smith, Warren B. *False Christ Coming: Does Anybody Care?: What New Age Leaders Really Have in Store for America, the Church, and the World.* Magalia, CA: Mountain Stream Press, 2011, section, 1148, 1445, 1463, 2400

Admin, Berean. "NAR Prophets Claim the Three Streams Will Be One." Berean Research, February 1, 2017. https://bereanresearch.org/nar-prophets-claim-three-streams-will-one/.

Strom, Andrew. *Kundalini Warning: Are False Spirits Invading the Church?*United States: Revival School, 2015, Pg. 24, 58

Teichrib, Carl. *Game of Gods: the Temple of Man in the Age of Re-Enchantment.* Place of publication not identified: Whitemud House Publishing, 2018, Pg. 393, 411

Vivekananda, Swami. *The Yoga Sutras of Patanjali.* Publisher unknown, n.d., Section 818, 941, 961, 1020, 1135, 1896

| C. Peter Wagner Explains The New Apostolic Reformation. Accessed January 23, 2020. http://www.talk2action.org/story/2009/5/28/19033/8502.

Weldon, John. jashow.org. Accessed January 23, 2020. https://www.jashow.org/articles/yoga-the-occult/.

Yungen, Ray. *A Time of Departing: How a Universal Spirituality Is Changing the Face of Christianity.* Eureka, MT: Lighthouse Trails Pub., 2006, Pg. 134, 147

Yungen, Ray. "NEW BOOKLET: Alice Bailey, the Mother of the New Age Movement And Her Plans to 'Revitalize' Christianity." Lighthouse Trails Inc, June 7, 2016. https://www.lighthousetrailsresearch.com/blog/?p=20753.

Berkley Center for Religion, and Georgetown University. "Swami Vivekananda on Truth in All Religions in Welcoming Participants to the World Parliament of Religions." Berkley Center for Religion, Peace and World Affairs. Accessed January 24, 2020. https://berkleycenter.georgetown.edu/quotes/swami-vivekananda-on-truth-in-all-religions-in-welcoming-participants-to-the-world-parliament-of-religions.

Divination Finds Further Expression In The Evangelical Church. Accessed January 24, 2020. http://www.deceptioninthechurch.com/divinationfindsfurtherexpression.html.

Manifest Sons of God. Accessed January 24, 2020. http://www.letusreason.org/Latrain1.htm.

"The New Group of World Servers - Key Concepts (Lucis Trust)." Lucis Trust. Accessed January 24, 2020. https://www.lucistrust.org/world_goodwill/key_concepts/the_new_group_world_servers3.

"Swami Vivekananda's Birthday." Shepparton Interfaith Network. Accessed 2020. Sheppartoninterfaith.org.au.

"Shaktipat Initiation." Welcome to the Siddha Yoga path. Accessed January 24, 2020. https://www.siddhayoga.org/shaktipat-spiritual-initiation.

"Trust Your Instincts." Svarasa. Accessed January 24, 2020. http://www.svarasa.com/.

Made in the USA
Las Vegas, NV
24 August 2021

28802595R00107